The Perfect Interview

The Perfect Interview

How to Get the Job You Really Want

John D. Drake

Second Edition

amacom
American Management Association
New York • Atlanta • Boston • Chicago • Kansas City • San Francisco • Washington, D.C.
Brussels • Mexico City • Tokyo • Toronto

This book is available at a special discount when ordered in bulk quantities. For information, contact Special Sales Department, AMACOM, a division of American Management Association, 1601 Broadway, New York, NY 10019.

Library of Congress Cataloging-in-Publication Data

Drake, John D.
The perfect interview : how to get the job you really want / John D. Drake. — 2nd ed.
p. cm.
Includes bibliographical references (p.) and index.
ISBN 0-8144-7919-7
1. Employment interviewing. I. Title.
HF5549.5.I6D74 1996
650.14—dc20 *96–9327*
CIP

Printing number

10 9 8 7 6 5 4 3 2 1

For our sons:
Rob, Tim, Peter, and **John**

Contents

Introduction

When it comes to getting the job you want, successful interviews are absolutely essential. No matter how solid and impressive your background may be, the way you are perceived during your interviews will determine what will happen next—job offer or turndown.

What This Book Is All About

The Perfect Interview was written to help you get the job you really want—from gaining an interview appointment to negotiating your compensation. It shows you ways to take your unique qualities and talents and present them to make the best possible impression on any potential employer.

The techniques and concepts provided will be equally effective for first-time job hunters and for those who have been on many interviews.

The book is based upon my professional experience, including hundreds of interviews with job candidates at all levels—from hourly rated trainees to presidents of Fortune 500 companies. It also calls upon more than twenty years of hands-on experience in counseling individuals on the best ways to present themselves during employment interviews. I have tried to delineate here only those techniques and methods that I have directly observed to be practical and productive—ones that have actually proved successful in the job-hunting marketplace.

The Perfect Interview was written because, as a professional interviewer, I have repeatedly seen well-qualified candidates rejected for a job because they did not present themselves effectively during their interviews. In a sense, they hanged themselves. Sometimes it was simply a matter of talking too much; at other times they made comments that were self-defeating. Whatever the case, it was clear to me that, with adequate training, they could easily have avoided almost every mistake I observed.

When I examined other books about going on employment interviews, I was disappointed. Very few existed; those that were available usually focused on one narrow aspect of interviewing, such as grooming and dress. Others provided sound recommendations such as "be consistent," but they did not furnish specific steps that would enable the reader to avoid being inconsistent.

Another problem was that most of the books were designed for passive learning. Unfortunately, acquiring good interviewing skills requires active practice and organized preparation. If you are like most people, frankly discussing your strengths in an employment interview is not something that comes naturally. For instance, how would you respond right now if an interviewer said, "Tell me about yourself"? Without experimenting with answers to such questions, failure in real-life interviews is highly probable.

The Perfect Interview was written in an effort to avoid shortcomings such as these. In essence, I have attempted to show you how to present your strengths most effectively during many different kinds of employment interviews.

How This Book Is Organized

The book follows the same chronological pattern that occurs during the interview process itself. That is, it describes what to do *before, during,* and *after* the interview.

The Perfect Interview also includes practice exercises that will enable you to acquire all the skills necessary for managing yourself successfully during various stages of the interview process. The exercises, called Skill Builders, are a most important feature of this book. They are designed to be practical and interesting and to help you gain confidence in handling interviews. Quite likely they will help you with new and interesting insights about yourself.

Even if, after an interview, you are not offered the job, this book will teach you to profit from the interview experience. It will help you analyze why you weren't successful and guide you to becoming an even more attractive candidate during your next interview.

It is my sincere wish that this book will help you conduct the "perfect interview" and win the job you really want.

John D. Drake
Kennebunkport, Maine

Acknowledgments

I would like to thank my wife, Delia, for her creative ideas for improving the text. I am grateful to Jurg Oppliger for contributing his extensive outplacement experience to Section One. I also want to express my thanks to Sebastian Milardo and Ray Inglesi, my partners at Drake Inglesi Milardo, Inc., for their helpful recommendations based on their professional interviewing experience. My hat is tipped to author/consultant John Lucht for his constant encouragement of and enthusiasm for *The Perfect Interview*.

Section One

Creative Techniques for Getting an Interview

Chapter 1

Getting an Interview: What Works, What Doesn't

This book is about making a great impact during your employment interviews. But before you can make that impact, you must first find someone who is willing to interview you.

Here's a possible scenario: You're looking for a job. You call a friend who knows Carolyn Johnson in XYZ Corporation's human resources department. You call Ms. Johnson and she invites you in for an interview. Possible? Yes. Probable? Not by a long shot.

The Realities

If you're job hunting, it's helpful to recognize that you already have a full-time job. Lining up interviews and finding a new position usually requires effort—lots of it. In a word, it's a "numbers game." It's much like selling: If you make enough calls, eventually you will make a sale. An experienced salesperson may even be able to tell you that it takes X number of calls to make Y number of sales.

And so it is with getting an interview. The more people you contact, the more likely it is that an interview will result. You need to plan for conducting a substantial campaign; making over 100 contacts is not excessive.

The question is, what kind of efforts are most productive in producing an interview? That's what this section is all about.

Some Basics

Where are the jobs? Jobs can be found in two basic arenas:

1. The public job market
2. The hidden job market

The Public Job Market

This market consists of all the jobs that are openly proclaimed. We learn about them through ads in newspapers and magazines or from employment agencies or executive search firms.

The Hidden Job Market

This market represents all the jobs that are not publicly announced. Sometimes these jobs haven't even been identified yet by the prospective employer. It's a key market because more than half the jobs filled stem from this arena. Some of them are filled by the company's own employees, some by the employer's network, but many are filled by persons like you who appear at "the right place at the right time."

Where's the Best Place to Look?

Drake Beam Morin, Inc. (DBM), the world's largest career transition company, helps thousands of men and women worldwide to find new jobs. They say of the people who work with them that:

- 70 percent find jobs through *networking* (hidden job market).
- 15 percent find jobs through *search firms/employment agencies* (public job market).
- 10 percent find jobs through *targeted letters* (hidden job market).
- 5 percent find jobs through *answering ads* (public job market).

The amazing finding is that 80 percent of these jobs came via the hidden job market. So, while we can't ignore advertisements and the public job market when we're seeking interviews, it is clear that our efforts can most productively be focused on the hidden market. It's to this market that we'll pay the most attention in this section.

Chapter 2

The Public Job Market: How to Get Interviews

Even though the likelihood of getting an interview invitation via the public job market is low, you can't ignore publicized openings—whether you learn about them from contacts with employment agencies, search firms, or advertisements. In this chapter, we'll discuss this market and pinpoint what's best to do and how to do it.

Answering Employment Advertisements

The least productive effort for gaining an interview is responding to employment ads. Even so, answering ads should be part of your daily job-hunting routine. There is always the possibility that your response will be well received and you'll be invited for an interview. In addition, perusing employment ads provides useful input on companies that are expanding or in a hiring mode. You can then approach these organizations using hidden job market techniques (as discussed in Chapter 3).

When answering ads, it's important not to get discouraged by the absence of a positive reply (or a reply of any kind, for that matter). It is not unusual for an ad to generate 200 or more résumés for the employer to review.

It's helpful to recognize that your ad response can easily get lost in the shuffle. Whoever reviews the ad responses will typically conduct a rapid screening and eliminate all those who do not closely match the job requirements.

Your challenge is to get into the "to be considered further" pile of résumés. The key here is to send a response that *quickly* reveals that you have what the ad has asked for.

Gaining the Competitive Edge When Answering Ads

1. *Read the ad carefully and highlight every specification or requirement the ad mentions.* An example, which might have appeared in *The Wall Street*

Journal, is shown in Figure 2-1. I have italicized the words that you would normally highlight.

2. *Prepare a covering letter that explains how you can deliver on the stated specs.* Don't be concerned if the ad asks for five qualifications and you have only three. Remember, the employer is painting a picture of the "ideal" candidate and may have to make some concessions to fill the vacancy. Focus only on the highlighted issues. The rest of your background can be shown in your accompanying résumé.

Three key elements will give impact to your cover letter:

a. *Brevity*—no more than one page.
b. *Word choice*—use of the same words to describe your qualifications as you found in the ad. Remember, they are important to the ad writer and hiring organization.
c. *Typewritten*—on good white bond. Sometimes handwritten letters attract attention, but more often they're not read because handwriting is usually more demanding to read than type.

Figure 2-2 gives an example of a cover letter written in response to the ad shown in Figure 2-1.

Even though the ad did not give the human resources director's

Figure 2-1. Newspaper ad for manufacturing position available.

PLANT MANAGER

Plastic container manufacturer is seeking a *career-oriented professional* for the position of Plant Manager in our Charleston, WV plant. The candidate should be an *aggressive "hands on" professional* with *5–7 years plant-level manufacturing experience,* preferably *in the plastic molding industry.*

This individual will be responsible for all operations at this facility and should *possess good technical training skills,* along with a *strong management background.* BA/BS helpful.

A competitive salary, a full range of benefits, and excellent opportunities for career growth await the right person.

Please reply by submitting your resume and salary requirements to:

Human Resources Dept.
ABC Plastics, Inc.
100 Smokestack Road
Wheeling, WV 25000

Figure 2-2. Response to open ad for plant manager.

Robert A. Smith, Director
Human Resources Dept.
ABC Plastics, Inc.
100 Smokestack Road
Wheeling, WV 25000

Dear Mr. Smith:

In a recent issue of *The Wall Street Journal,* you advertised for a Plant Manager for your Charleston, WV operation. I believe I meet all your requirements:

You Want	*I Can Offer*
Aggressive "hands on" professional	I "work the floor." Manage by roaming. Not afraid to get my hands dirty or get into equipment.
5–7 yrs. plant level exp. in plastic molding	Four years at Universal Plastics in management, process engineering, and quality. Two years at Allied as plant manager.
Good technical skills	BS in Chem. Engineering plus 6 years plastic molding exp. with containers, building materials, and custom work.
Strong managerial background	Managed a 300-employee plant; served as Ass't Plant Manager in 125-employee plant.

The enclosed résumé provides additional data about my qualifications. Salary requirements are flexible, depending upon opportunity.

I look forward to hearing from you.

Sincerely yours,

name, the cover letter is addressed to Mr. Smith, the human resources director. Whenever possible, write to a specific person. Names can be gleaned from business directories, as listed in the "Sources" section at the end of this book, and/or by calling the company directly and asking for the name.

3. *Customize your résumé.* It will be helpful if your résumé also emphasizes the job qualifications that were highlighted in the ad. If it doesn't, sometimes a minor "tuning" is all that is required. If revision is impractical, send your résumé as is. But if extensive revision is needed, you are probably going after the wrong job.

Getting Interviews With Employment Agencies

It is relatively easy to get an interview appointment at an employment agency because agencies are always seeking job applicants. The more people they see, the more likely it is that they'll find an acceptable candidate and earn their placement commission.

Gaining the Competitive Edge With Employment Agencies

1. *Be selective.* It's a question of quality. Better, longer-established agencies with more professional staff tend to get job openings from the best employers. However, it is not always a matter of agency size. Once in a while a small, one- or two-person agency is the best in town.

There is also the privacy issue. Less reputable agencies may scatter your résumé so widely that your privacy and reputation are at risk.

One of the best ways to learn about an agency's reputation is to ask people who have used it. Ask around. Helpful input can also be gleaned from someone you know in human resources in the agency's city.

2. *Use the phone/fax.* You can save time and effort by calling or faxing to see if the agency has a match between your background and the jobs it is trying to fill. This approach is most effective for positions at the $30,000 to $75,000 level.

The afternoon is the best time for faxing or phone calls; in most agencies, mornings are too hectic. E-mail is acceptable, too, if the agency has an on-line address.

How much should you communicate?

My experience is that something brief and to the point is more likely to get attention than a communication offering much detail. Since the agency needs you as much as you need it, the agency can always ask for more information if you are a possible "fit."

What should you communicate?

Mention the essentials. Here are some items that are almost always appropriate:

1. Kind of job(s) you are looking for, e.g., engineering, bookkeeping, fashion design
2. Full, part-time, or either type of employment
3. Highest educational attainments
4. Key job experiences

Figure 2-3 shows an example of a FAX/e-mail to an agency.

Getting Interviews With Executive Search Firms

Most professional executive recruiters, unlike employment agencies, work on a retainer basis. Their clients pay them 30 percent or more of the base salary attached to the opening to find the right candidate. The expectation is that the professional recruiter will search out individuals who are highly successful in their present positions. For this reason, retainer search firms are hardly ever interested in "walk-ins."

There are, however, "executive search" firms that work on a contingency basis. These can be managed in the same manner as employment agencies.

For the reasons just cited, it is usually not worth investing your time with retainer search firms unless:

1. You are earning $75,000 or more.
2. You are currently employed.
3. You personally know someone in the search firm.

Unless you meet these minimal requirements, the odds of your getting even a "courtesy" interview are slim.

Despite these caveats, search firms are still worth pursuing if you meet the following requirements:

1. You know someone who knows someone in the search firm. This could be an individual the firm previously placed or an executive whose company employs the search firm.
2. You've been a highly successful performer but are "out looking" because of an impending downsizing or merger.
3. You are or were a senior executive in a well-known or highly regarded firm and are recognized in your industry.
4. You are/were making more than $75,000 a year.

Figure 2-3. Brief initial communication stressing qualifications.

Quick Find Agency
234 Main Street
Anytown, USA

Re: Position in *Data Processing* or *Information Services*

Qualifications

- Six years' experience in PC network environment
- Work with: Windows, DOS, Unix, Novell
- Know: database management and programming

BS Computer Sciences, University of Maine

I am an enthusiastic professional who has successfully managed a data processing department. I am team-oriented and can gain quick acceptance from my clients.

Flexible on salary, depending upon opportunity.

I will call in a few days to see if my qualifications meet your needs. In the meantime, if you wish more data, I can be reached at: (207) 444-5555 or JJONES@AOL.

John Jones
123 Elm Avenue
Somewhere, ME 04000

Gaining the Competitive Edge With Executive Search Firms

1. *Get in touch with a lot of recruiters.* Whether or not a recruiter asks you in for an interview depends largely on the existence of a potential match between you and the searches the firm is currently conducting. The more firms you contact, the better your chances are. Don't overlook

the smaller ones. For a comprehensive list of recruiters, obtain a copy of *Directory of Executive Recruiters* (see Sources).

2. *Exploit every opportunity to establish a personal contact in the search firms you write.* Large search firms receive hundreds of résumés each day. Unless someone in that firm is specifically looking for your résumé, the probability of its being carefully read is slim. Whom do you know who knows someone working in executive search? If one of your friends knows a recruiter, get permission to use his or her name when writing to that recruiter.

3. *Make contact with search firms long before you're ready to make a move.* You are a more attractive candidate when you need to be ''coaxed'' out of a current assignment.

3. *Don't send a ''cutesy'' cover letter or résumé.* Address your cover letter to a specific person and design it so that it briefly describes your current work and a few significant achievements. Your main objective is to get the recruiter to turn the page and examine your résumé. Your résumé should be complete and chronological and it should highlight your achievements in quantitative terms.

It is beyond the scope of this book to provide techniques for writing cover letters and résumés.

4. *Read John Lucht's book,* Rites of Passage at $100,000+. Lucht is an executive search professional who provides expert advice on working with retainer recruiters.

Chapter 3

The Hidden Job Market: Getting Your Interviews

The hidden job market consists of positions that are not publicly posted; they are not advertised or listed with either employment agencies or executive search firms.

These jobs exist for a number of reasons. Sometimes a position has just opened up, but the company hasn't yet begun formal efforts at replacement (someone resigned, for example). Some exist because the company is attempting to fill them from within. Still other jobs are open, but the formal hiring "OK" has not yet been given. In each of these situations, an interview is likely to occur if the right résumé suddenly appears. That résumé could be yours!

In Chapter 1, I mentioned how a major outplacement firm found that 70 percent of its placements stemmed from *networking* versus only 10 percent from *direct mail*. The evidence seems clear: The most productive use of your interview-seeking time lies in cultivating the hidden job marketplace. Because networking is so essential in this arena, we'll start with that.

Networking: What It's All About

The idea behind networking is simple. To get a job offer, you need to be interviewed by someone who has a position you want. But it's not easy to locate people who have the jobs, much less get an interview, *unless* you know individuals who are hiring or know someone who knows them and is willing to refer you. That's what networking is all about—using your contacts to set up interviews with potential employers and/or to add new names of people with whom to network.

So what's new? It's obvious that if you want to find a new job, you talk with people who may have the kind of job you want. But therein lies the problem. Most of us have a rather limited number of such contacts and, as we shall see, approaching them directly for a job is often fraught with difficulties.

For a perspective on these problems, let's see how it plays out from your contact's viewpoint. Suppose I once worked with you at Generic Foods. You left GF to seek greener pastures, but I stayed on. You call me, and after the polite "How have you been?" preliminaries, you tell me that you have been caught in a downsizing at Generic Mills and you're wondering what might be available at GF.

Before I respond to your question, I quickly recall that I liked you when we worked together but nevertheless always thought you were a little pushy. I am also aware that my boss still harbors some negative feelings about your leaving us. For an instant, I consider the political implications of advocating your return to GF. I wonder what you've been doing these past three years and if you've changed any. I realize that if I invite you in so we can get reacquainted, it might set up false expectations and become a little awkward for me if I can't then offer you anything. Because I feel uncertain about what commitment to make, and also because I'm so busy, I respond:

> "I'm so sorry to hear about your situation. I read about the downsizing last week in *The Wall Street Journal*. I really wish I could help you, Jason, but as you know, we too are staying 'mean and lean,' and at the moment, we're not adding to staff. . . ."

The reality is that I would like to be of help, it might even be fun to work together again, but my uncomfortable feelings influence my response. I will probably suggest that you send me a résumé and tell you that "I'll keep an eye open." Even though we end our conversation on a pleasant note, the net effect is no interview for you.

The lesson we learn from this typical situation is that it is risky to ask for a job from those you know. The solution is to network.

How It Works

Most often, networking is accomplished by calling someone you know for the purpose of getting an interview to discuss one or more of the following:

- Your contact's thoughts about career changes you are considering
- Opportunities in the industry
- Advice as to who would be useful to contact
- The possibility of help in gaining an interview with a targeted company or individual.

Notice, at no time is it even implied that you are looking to your contact for a job.

In a nutshell, networking is effective because it gets you interviews. You gain direct access to potential employers because asking for advice, instead of a job, minimizes your contact's tendency to become defensive. Your contact may even be flattered that you are calling and asking for some help.

Advantages

There are several potential benefits from following this indirect route:

1. Your contact may realize that you might qualify for an opening in his own firm.
2. Your contact may know of an opening in another firm that matches your background.
3. Your contact may provide the names of, or introduce you to, others with whom you can network or talk with directly about a job.
4. Your contact may provide helpful advice and guidance that enhances your job search.

Disadvantages

While it is true that networking has the potential to geometrically expand your possibilities for job interviews, the method has its limitations:

1. It takes a lot of time. At best, you'll be able to schedule only two or three interviews a day. At that rate, it could take several months to find the right person with the right job.
2. It becomes expensive and time-consuming to conduct networking interviews beyond a convenient travel distance. Consequently, networking is not a practical technique for finding the best job on a national or international basis.
3. Networking is arduous. Not knowing how your initial call will be received is often anxiety-provoking; following up on referrals can be tedious and painful. Trying to get past secretaries or learning that your contact is almost always "out of town" can be very frustrating.

Even though networking may not be the ideal approach in some circumstances, it remains a key way to get employment interviews. Let's examine how it's done.

Contacts: Where Networking Starts

To get a the hidden job market, you need a broad contact base. This requires work, but once you've established a plan of action, it's not all that difficult.

The first step is to establish a *contact list.* Start it by thinking about people you already know; then use them to help expand your list. Think of everyone you know who has direct contacts with potential employers or who may know someone who has such contacts. Here are a few sources that can provide names for beginning your list:

- Work associates, past and present
- Family and friends; your Christmas card list and personal phone book can be great sources.
- Professional and business organizations. Membership directories can often help you to recall names and also provide a convenient source of addresses and phone numbers.
- Social contacts in clubs and recreational activities.
- Members of your religious or community organizations
- Your college alumni directory and college placement office
- Old school friends, teachers, and professors
- Merchants and suppliers
- Professionals such as:
  —Lawyers
  —Accountants
  —Bankers
  —Real estate brokers
  —Editors of trade journals or writers of articles
  —Stockbrokers
  —Insurance agents
  —Congresspeople

Organizing Your Contact List

An efficient way to keep track of your network names is to place each one on a 3 × 5 index card. These cards provide adequate space for addresses, phone numbers, and notes, but flexibility is their advantage over notebooks. Cards are easy to sort into piles headed "call back tomorrow," "send résumé," and "no further interest."

Figure 3-1 shows a card layout that our clients have found useful.

Your local print shop can inexpensively print your blank file cards with this or a similar layout. In any case, you will need some system for keeping track of each phone call, letter, interview, follow-up, and prom-

Figure 3-1. Networking card form for furthering the job search.

[*Front*]

Name ____________________ Tel #(   ) ____________________

Company ____________________ Title ____________________

Address ____

Date of Int. / /   We discussed: ____________________

____

____

____

[*Back*]

Referred to:

Name ____________________ Tel #(   ) ____________________

Company ____________________ Title ____________________

Comments ____

Name ____________________ Tel #(   ) ____________________

Company ____________________ Title ____________________

Comments ____

ise. Without one, your job-hunting campaign can quickly become muddled and result in much wasted time.

Using Your Contact List

Obviously, not everyone on your list is going to be worth contacting. The problem is, until you ask, you really won't know who has the right connections or who will be of help.

You might judge, for example, that your local dentist is unlikely to have contacts with the president of a targeted company located a thousand miles away. But perhaps her college sorority sister is a VP in that company. You just never know. Unfortunately, time limitations usually make it necessary for you to prioritize your contact list. Here are a few ways to do it:

How to Prioritize Your List

1. As specifically as you can, define your *target locations, industries,* or *organizations*. For example, "I want to stay in the Southwest, in aerospace, and work for a major 'player.' " Your target can be further refined by delineating three or four specific companies that fit the bill. At the end of this chapter, you can use Skill Builder 1 to help organize your targets.

2. As you consider calling each contact, ask yourself this question: "What is the likelihood that this person knows someone in my target areas?" If you judge the probability is 50 percent or more, make the call and network. However, if you are getting an insufficient number of interviews, you may have to lower your probability figure to 30–40 percent or broaden your target base.

It's not just a question of dutifully making calls on a list, however. You want to maximize the benefits that your contacts may be able to provide.

Gaining the Competitive Edge in Networking

Here are a few tips to help make your networking pay off:

1. *Plan and rehearse key parts of your initial telephone call, especially your opening comments.* Without such preparation, your call to a former colleague could sound like this:

> "Hi, Jeff. I'm sorry to trouble you, but I'm in a bit of a bind. Last week I got caught in our company's downsizing, and so I'm out looking for another position."

How do you think Jeff will react to this desperate scenario? How would you react? If you are like most of us, your defenses will be raised and you'll be thinking: "How can I gracefully extricate myself from this situation?"

So, before you pick up the phone, outline what you are going to say and prepare how you will react to the responses you receive.

To assist you in planning your networking call, consult the step-by-step model provided at the conclusion of this list of networking suggestions.

2. *Make your first few networking calls with the least important names on your list.* It takes some practice to find the most effective ways of presenting yourself; you don't want to experiment with your best contacts.

3. *In both meetings and phone calls keep an eye on the clock.* Never use more time than you have asked for unless it's offered spontaneously and voluntarily.

4. *Keep your contacts abreast of where their suggestions have led and of how their referrals panned out.* Keep it brief and chatty. For instance:

> "You made the suggestion that I talk with Sam Jenkins. Well, when I was in his office, I got introduced to his data processing manager, Bill Byte, and he was quite interested in how I set up our new warehouse inventory system. We're going to meet again next Friday."

5. *Before concluding your network interview, determine how you can follow up on it without being too pushy or overbearing.* Without some easy way to check on progress, you could easily assume that your contact's promise to help was actually realized, whereas, in reality, nothing has been done.

If, for example, your contact indicates that she will mention you to Mr. Bigwig, you might say:

> "That would be great!" Should I wait a week before I follow up with him or would it be best if I touched base with you first to see how it went?"

Sometimes it's helpful to have a generic phrase handy to involve your contact in how best to follow up. Here are a few:

> "What do you think would be our next step?"
>
> "How should we handle it from here on out?"
>
> "Does it make any sense to you if I . . . ?"

6. *Increase your impact on targeted organizations by using sponsors.* If your networking contacts have stature in their respective industries, consider asking them to be a sponsor. In short, you ask a sponsor to write letters recommending you.

Since you can't expect your sponsor to go to the trouble of developing, printing, and mailing these letters, you, of course, must take care of these tasks. Your sponsor may even ask that you sign them with his signature.

Since the sponsoring letter will explain how capable and talented you are, it will also need to provide a clear explanation as to why the sponsor is not hiring you. This is not too difficult to explain unless your sponsor is the chief executive of a large corporation having many divisions in which you could be placed.

Figure 3-2 reproduces a sponsoring letter that produced a new job for one of my clients:

A Step-by-Step Procedure for Making Networking Calls

One way to plan your initial phone call is to think of it as having four steps, each one naturally flowing to the next. Here they are:

Step 1. Before Dialing

Determine the objective of your call. Exactly what do you hope to accomplish: Set up an interview date? Send a résumé? Convey your availability? Be clear in your own mind and also have a fallback objective in case you do not gain your first.

What will you do, for example, if your contact declines your request for a brief interview but instead offers to "talk right now"? Given the current extensive use of networking, this reaction is quite likely.

It is our experience that it's usually best to accept your contact's willingness to talk a while on the phone. Once such an offer is extended, the odds are slim that you'll be granted a face-to-face interview. Sometimes, during telephone conversations, you can generate sufficient interest that your contact himself suggests that "we get together."

Keep at hand a blank contact card and your appointment calendar while you are talking.

Be relaxed. It is most important that you begin on a positive note—both in the words you use and the feelings you convey. If you come across as anxious or panicky, your upbeat words will mean little. If you feel tense, don't dial. Take a few deep breaths and exhale slowly. If this doesn't result in calmness, try to pinpoint the cause of your anxiety and "talk it out" (with yourself or someone else). For example, if the source of the tension is your fear of being rejected, you may find it helpful to mull over the fact that networking will always produce some rejections. Perhaps the call you're about to make will be one of them—it's part of the game. You win a few, lose a few.

Figure 3-2. Example of a sponsoring letter.

ELECTRONIC SPECIALTIES, INC.
800 Diode Avenue
Silicon, CA 99999
(802) 967-5000

Charles Smith, CEO
Components Unlimited, Inc.
100 Park Street
Chicago, IL 77777

Dear Mr. Smith:

Over the years, I have found that it is easy to recruit competent professionals who were competent in human resources. Most of them, however, didn't know the electronics business nor distinguish themselves as members of our management team.

Last week, I learned about the availability of a human resources executive who is unlike those I have just described. This man helped me develop our business from $3 million to nearly $200 million. He was not simply a staff executive, but was as much involved in running our business as our production and sales VPs were. He is bright and personable and has exceptional business savvy.

Unfortunately, I lost him after five years to an executive recruiter who dangled too big a "carrot." Currently, he is with the firm that recruited him, but this company has now been acquired by a Fortune 500 firm that seems intent on bringing in its own team.

Since he is still solidly employed, I must keep his name in confidence. I'd have him back here, except that I recently appointed a new, up-from-the-ranks VP of Human Resources and to unseat her right now would be grossly unfair.

While he indicates that finding a dynamic, growing organization is a high priority, you should know that his total compensation for the past three years has ranged from $110,000 to $175,000.

If you are interested in a human resources executive who really knows the electronics industry, I'd be pleased to put you in touch with him.

Sincerely yours,

Charles T. Wyman
President

CW:mm
Enclosure

Step 2. Opening Remarks

Plan what you will say to "connect" with your contact. Think of your opening remarks as "bonding comments." It's usually best to be brief and straightforward. For example, when calling a former employer with whom you've been out of touch for ten years, you might start by simply saying:

> "Hello Martha, this is ______________, I wonder if you remember me. I was head of accounts payable when you were VP of Finance over at XYZ Company. . . ."

It is usually best to keep small talk to a minimum. Opening your conversation with extended chitchat often creates tension as your contact awaits the purpose of your call.

When calling old friends, it is often a temptation to reminisce about "old times," and while that may be enjoyable, you need to recognize that your contact is at work and likely to be busy. The bonding in these calls stems from the warmth and informality of your opening remarks. For example:

You Hi Miles, this is ______________. Are you up to your neck in work?

Miles: John, I could use a couple of days with fifty hours in them. . . .

You: Look, I won't keep you but a minute. I just wanted to see if you'd be free for lunch sometime next week. I'd like to pick your brains. . . .

Here is a generic opening that will fit most situations:

You: Hi ______________.[*Add here whatever* brief *introductory comments seem appropriate.*] I have decided to make a change in my career and I'm beginning to look at opportunities in ABC and XYZ companies. I know you must be busy, but I was wondering if you could give me fifteen minutes so I can get your input about ______________."
[a, b, or c]

a. My job search strategies
b. People I'm thinking about contacting
c. People you might know

We need to recognize, too, that with outplacement firms advocating networking, the person you reach may already have received many networking calls. Your contact may be well aware that you're not simply calling for advice or information but hoping, in many cases, that he or she might be a source of employment.

For this reason, you may find your initial call more welcomed if you are open about your intentions. For example:

You: Brian, I'm going to be right up front with you. The reason I'm making this call is because I'm doing some networking. I've decided to make a career change and I'm looking to make some contacts in the ______________ industry. I know that you've been in that arena for a long time and I was wondering if you could give me fifteen minutes to talk about it."

Step 3. Listening

Once you have made your opening request, it is essential that you now be silent and carefully listen to your contact's response. If it is positive, move quickly. Thank your contact for his willingness to help and "nail down" the next step. For instance:

You: OK, I've got my calendar here, how would next Tuesday be?

[*or*]

I'll put my résumé in the mail today.

If your contact's response is cool or negative, try to mirror back your understanding of the resistance. In this way, you can both look at the obstacle objectively and increase the likelihood that a problem-solving discussion will ensue. Such an exchange may help overcome the barrier. Here's an example:

Contact: I'd be happy to talk with you, but I'm going to be "out flat" for the next couple of weeks.

You: Finding the fifteen minutes is really a problem for you right now. . . .

Contact: Yeah, John, this is our busy season and I don't see how I can take time out . . . except maybe for lunch . . . that might work out. How about a quick lunch next week?

Step 4. Closing

Quite often the closing is a simple matter of expressing appreciation for the time given and for whatever assistance was offered.

At other times, nothing is promised. In these situations you may still wish to keep the contact alive by offering to send your résumé, "in case you see a situation that might be appropriate for me."

This networking call format is provided as a general guideline. It needs to be adapted to your personality and style as well as to your contact's responses. Skill Builder 2 will help you prepare for these important telephone calls.

Direct Mail: What It's All About

The value of direct mail is closely related to the number of potential employers you contact. The more the better. John Lucht, in *Rites of Passage at $100,000+*, provides this formula for a successful direct mail campaign:

> Send 1,000 letters . . . not less.
>
> Expect to receive three to five affirmative replies . . . not more.
>
> If you do it right, those five or six meaningful replies should lead to three or four interviews and two or three offers of exactly what you want.

Of course, it's a big task, and at times it will become tedious. But once you get into the flow of it, direct mail can be an absorbing challenge. You are likely to find that during the process of determining which potential employers to write, you will define, more precisely, what you want from your next position.

Another advantage of direct mail is that it allows you to target whatever is most important to you. You can focus on specific industries or organizations in any location you choose.

Gaining the Competitive Edge When Using Direct Mail

Of all the factors involved in direct mail, the most important is the quality of the letter you write. Remember that outplacement firms typically encourage and assist their clients in conducting direct mail campaigns. Consequently, key officers in major organizations are often inundated with letters from individuals seeking employment. For your letter to be looked at, it must be outstanding.

How to Make Your Cover Letter Stand Out

1. *Address it to a particular person*—someone who is two levels or more above your target job. It's better to err on the side of sending it too high in the organization than too low.

2. *Be sure that the name, title, and address are correct.* This is not much of a problem when mailing to persons whose names were obtained via networking, but it can be with names generated from business directories. Even directories with the current year on their covers are suspect; they were, after all, assembled during the previous year. With today's almost endless downsizings, restructurings, and reorganizations, the bet is that at least one-third of the directory names will be wrong. The only way to determine if the person you are writing to is still in control of the job you want is to call the organization and check it out. This is one task you might want to delegate to someone else.

3. *Keep it brief*—no more than one page.

4. *Focus on one or two clear, meaningful achievements.* Describe them in such a way that the reader can easily infer how your talents could be helpful. For example:

"During the past two years, I built, from scratch, a national sales force that successfully brought a new micro switch to the market. In the second year, we generated $2.3 million in sales."

5. *Mention your compensation.* If your potential employer is at all interested in your qualifications, the next question he will ask himself is, "Is this person in the ballpark?" Current compensation is the single most important factor in categorizing a candidate's appropriateness for a position.

Sometimes people say to me, "John, isn't that awfully risky? My compensation needs might rule me out of a job because I mentioned an amount that's too high."

This problem can be readily resolved by providing an acceptable compensation range. Use phraseology such as: "Although other factors such as [*fill in your own nonfinancial "turn-ons"*] are of primary importance, you should know that, in recent years, my total compensation has been in the range of ______________ to ______________." Make the bottom number the smallest amount you are willing to accept, the higher number your *total* compensation for your best year including all benefits, pensions, options, and perks.

6. *Don't say . . .*

- That you will call them. If they're interested, they will call you.
- You're willing to relocate. You wouldn't be writing to them if you weren't willing to move there.
- How great you are. Everyone knows you're biased. Words such as *results-oriented* or *analytically minded* are superfluous. Let your achievements speak for you.

Now that you have your basic letter designed, consider these five tips for getting your direct mail campaign under way.

1. *Start with companies that have an obvious fit with your talents and are located in your preferred geographical region.* When these organizations have been covered, extend your mailings to less relevant and less favorable locations. When selecting organizations, don't overlook the nonprofit sector, which includes foundations, institutions of learning, industry associations, and government. The directories listed in the "Sources" section of this book can help you compile your list. Most of them are available in your public library.

2. *Mail all of your 1,000 letters as fast as you can get them out.* There is no benefit from taking a "wait and see" approach to the first 100 or so letters you send. By the time you discover that no one has replied to your first batch, you will have wasted two or more weeks. Don't worry about having too much to follow up on; it's not likely that you'll get more than six positive responses.

3. *Start your direct mail campaign at the beginning of your job search.* It takes time to get rolling on a project of this sort, and little is gained by waiting.

4. *Consider mailing 2,000 letters.*

5. *Avoid gimmicks like colored paper or fancy fonts.* Use quality bond, with your name and address engraved or printed at the top. Your accompanying résumé should have the same conservative, no-nonsense appearance.

In summary, to get interviews that lead to jobs, use all the resources available to you—advertisements, employment agencies, executive search firms, networking, and direct mail. The effective job campaign includes time for each potential job source but allocates most of the effort to direct mail and networking.

Once you have an interview lined up, consult the remainder of this book for the tools and techniques that will enable you to convert that interview into a job offer.

SKILL BUILDER 1
Targeting Your Potential Employer

Your contact list is best used when you concentrate your energies on persons most likely to know someone who has the jobs you're seeking. This worksheet can help you establish those priorities.

1. TARGET LOCATIONS

In targeting locations, it is often worthwhile to think in terms of cities/towns and a 30-mile radius from their centers.

If you have no geographical preferences, skip to INDUSTRY TARGETS.

My #1 preference (city) ______________________
My #2 preference ______________________
My #3 preference ______________________
My #4 preference ______________________
My #5 preference ______________________

If you are open to locating anywhere within a broad geographic area, such as New England or France, write the names of these states or countries in the above spaces.

2. INDUSTRY TARGETS (for example, chemical, banking, retailing, real estate, advertising, etc.)

#1 choice ______________________
#2 choice ______________________
#3 choice ______________________
#4 choice ______________________

3. ORGANIZATION TARGETS (specific companies in which you would like to work)

#1 choice ______________________
#2 choice ______________________
#3 choice ______________________
#4 choice ______________________
#5 choice ______________________

SKILL BUILDER 2
Developing Your Networking Call

Planning your call will help you keep on focus and reduce anxiety during your first few calls. While each call may require an adjustment to fit the moment, having a planned format helps make it easier.

You might want to have this sheet in front of you as you make your first calls.

Step 1—*Before Dialing* (a few reminders)

__ contact card
__ appointment calendar
__ relaxed? Don't call until you are.

Step 2—*Opening Remarks*

- *What will you say to establish your relationship with the contact?*
- *What request are you going to make?*
- *What is your fallback request if your initial one is refused?*

A) **Friends**—Opening Words (Keep them brief, but warm and friendly.)

____

____

____

____

Now state your purpose(s)

__ Advice about career plan
__ Industry opportunities
__ Persons to contact
__ Interview with targeted individual or company

____

____

____

What is your ''fallback'' request? ______________________________

B) **Strangers**—Referrals from networking (Get networking referral name right up front.)

For example: ''Hello, ______________. My name is ______________, and I'm calling at the suggestion of ______________.''

Now state your purpose(s)
__ Advice about career plan
__ Industry opportunities
__ Persons to contact
__ Interview with targeted individual or company

____

____

____

____

What is your ''fallback'' request? ______________________________

C) **Former work associates** (Be specific about your past position and their relationship to you.)

____

____

____

Now state your purpose(s)
__ Advice about career plan
__ Industry opportunities
__ Persons to contact
__ Interview with targeted individual or company

____

____

____

____

What is your ''fallback'' request? ______________________________

Step 3—*Listening*

a) Don't argue. Paraphrase objections or any negative responses (''I see, you're concerned about . . .'').

b) If you get acceptance, don't prolong the conversation. ''Nail down'' the appointment date or some agreed upon next step.

Step 4—*Closing*

a) Express appreciation.

b) If nothing is promised, try to keep contact ''alive.'' Call again? Send résumé? What's best with this contact?

____

____

____

Section Two

Before the Interview: Getting Ready

Chapter 4

Learning About Your Prospective Employer

As a professional interviewer, I am constantly amazed at the number of job candidates who come to their interviews unprepared. This behavior is typically interpreted by interviewers as demonstrating a lack of good judgment. It often means no job offer. Successful interviews usually depend on good preparation. So let's start by looking at an important aspect of your preparation: knowing the company.

How Does Knowing the Company Help?

The more you know about the company at which you are interviewing, the more astute you are likely to be about the kinds of questions you ask the interviewer. But more important, knowledge of the company's products/services, profitability, customers, recent activities, or changes enables you to present your qualifications in such a way that you are likely to be perceived as a "good fit." Moreover, if you can learn about problems the company is experiencing, you may be able to explain how your skills could aid the organization's effort to deal with its difficulties.

Solid information about the company also can boost your confidence going into your interviews. Such knowledge provides an easy, and often impressive, common ground for discussion with your interviewers.

To help you organize and record information about each prospective employer, six *Company Fact Sheets* are provided in Skill Builder 3, at the end of this chapter. You will need a Fact Sheet for each company with which you'll be interviewing. Hopefully, you'll find these Fact Sheets convenient for organizing pertinent data. Armed with this material you can:

- Review important information on each company as you prepare for your interview (so that you'll know what questions to ask and how to highlight your strengths).

- Record your interviewer's reactions to what you said (so that you can learn and grow from your interview experience).
- Record names, addresses, and dates for follow-up actions you'll need to complete.

In addition, Figure 4-1 provides you with an example of an interview schedule sheet on which you can record each scheduled interview, with the name of the company, the interviewer, the time, and the location. This sheet provides both a way to keep track of your appointments and a quick means of reviewing those you've had.

Good Sources of Information About Organizations

There are a number of sources to which you can turn for up-to-date information on a company's activities and prospects. Some are official, some are highly unofficial, and all can be very useful.

Friends and Acquaintances

People you may know who currently work for the company where you are going to be interviewed or who used to work there can serve as excellent resources. Here are some questions you could ask them:

> "What is the corporate culture or work climate like?"
>
> "What are the organization's current successes and problems?"
>
> "What kind of person best fits in this company?"
>
> "What is the history of the company? How did it get where it is today?"
>
> "What are the names of people who make it happen there?"
>
> "What do they make or sell?"
>
> "What are the backgrounds of the key managers—especially in the department that interests me?"
>
> "Who are the organization's customers or clients?"

This personal, hands-on information about each prospective employer is often the most useful knowledge base of all. In addition to helping you know what to say about your qualifications, it provides you with a basis for making strong, honest statements about your desire to become a member of that organization. During an interview, you could say, for example:

> "I've spoken several times with Bill about his work here at ________________, and from what I've heard about the [chal-

Figure 4-1. Your interview schedule.

Date of Interview: __/__/__ :
Time: : A.M. P.M. ________ Organization ________ Location ________ Name of Interviewer

Date of Interview: __/__/__ :
Time: : A.M. P.M. ________ Organization ________ Location ________ Name of Interviewer

Date of Interview: __/__/__ :
Time: : A.M. P.M. ________ Organization ________ Location ________ Name of Interviewer

Date of Interview: __/__/__ :
Time: : A.M. P.M. ________ Organization ________ Location ________ Name of Interviewer

Date of Interview: __/__/__ :
Time: : A.M. P.M. ________ Organization ________ Location ________ Name of Interviewer

Date of Interview: __/__/__ :
Time: : A.M. P.M. ________ Organization ________ Location ________ Name of Interviewer

Date of Interview: __/__/__ :
Time: : A.M. P.M. ________ Organization ________ Location ________ Name of Interviewer

Date of Interview: __/__/__ :
Time: : A.M. P.M. ________ Organization ________ Location ________ Name of Interviewer

Date of Interview: __/__/__ :
Time: : A.M. P.M. ________ Organization ________ Location ________ Name of Interviewer

Date of Interview: __/__/__ :
Time: : A.M. P.M. ________ Organization ________ Location ________ Name of Interviewer

Date of Interview: __/__/__ :
Time: : A.M. P.M. ________ Organization ________ Location ________ Name of Interviewer

lenges/growth opportunities], this is the kind of company I want to be with."

Annual Reports

Published each year by all publicly held companies, annual reports provide a wealth of information and will answer most of the questions listed above. Almost every annual report contains a letter from the chairman of the board; the report usually reflects the personality of the company and its intended direction. These reports can be obtained by calling the company's shareholder relations department. Also, most stockbrokers will be pleased to obtain a copy for you.

Financial Publications

There are many excellent sources of information about the current status of a company, its potential, and much inside information about its successes and failures. Two readily available financial publications are:

The Value Line Investment Survey, 711 Third Avenue, New York, N.Y. 10017.

S&P Investor's Kit, Standard and Poor's Corporation, 25 Broadway, P.O. Box 992, New York, N.Y. 10275.

Most stockbrokers subscribe to these investment services and will be willing to send you a copy of the publication's evaluation of a company. If you are embarking on an extensive job search, you can purchase a short-term subscription yourself. *The Value Line*, for example, can be purchased for ten weeks for under $100. As a subscriber, you will receive current information on most large publicly held companies. Standard & Poor's offers a similar, special-price subscription.

Directories

Your local public or college library carries large reference works that typically include factual information about corporations, including addresses, telephone numbers, names and titles of officers, annual sales, and products. A few of the more readily available directories are listed in the Sources section.

While you may not wish to spend a lot of time researching every company you expect to be interviewing with, the importance of acquiring some knowledge about each potential employer cannot be overestimated. By examining the data on the completed Company Fact Sheet shown in

Figure 4-2 you can easily imagine how this kind of information can help you feel more confident about entering the interview. It can also make it relatively easy to discuss how your capabilities might be useful to a particular company.

College Placement Offices, Employment Agencies, and Executive Search Firms

If the company you will be interviewing with also recruits on your college campus, the college placement office will undoubtedly have literature about it. Indeed, the placement director might have significant insights to share with what interviewers are looking for in candidates.

If you are being referred by an employment agency, your agency representative will have an outline of the job requirements; if the agency has done repeated work for the company, other helpful information, such as the names and characteristics of the company's interviewers, may also be available. Agency personnel will usually be quite cooperative in providing this information, since their fee depends upon your getting the job.

If you are being referred to a company by an executive search firm, you will undoubtedly be coached by your executive recruiter. The search consultant wants to be certain that you come across as a viable candidate; his reputation is on the line. To be sure you have all the information you need, bring one of your Company Fact Sheets to the next meeting with your recruiter.

I have discussed here the major sources of information about organizations where you may be interviewing. Having this information readily available and easy to discuss is an essential part of being prepared for each interview. The Company Fact Sheets can be very helpful in assisting you to succinctly organize this information.

Figure 4-2. Sample filled-in Company Fact Sheet.

Company Fact Sheet

— Preparing for your Interview —

Company Name: Software Systems Design, Inc.

Location: 500 Computer Drive, Portland, Maine 04101

Contacts: ***(People I know who work there or know the Company)***

Name: Sally Harrison Name: Fred Johnson

Tel #: 686-2194 Tel #: 773-6121

Kind of Business: ***(Products and/or Services)***

Computer Software + Computer Accessories (hardware)

Names of Some Typical Customers:

Apple	Data Gen	Super Computers
NEC	Wang	

Significant Facts:

Annual Sales Volume: $ 362,000,000

Growth Pattern (past 5 yrs.) very fast - have increased sales at near 50% rate for past 3 years

Number of Employees: 1,260 Headqtr. Location: Portland, Maine

Other Locations: San José, CA Raleigh, NC

Interesting Production Statistics: make all software for Super Computers; make over 85 software packages

Names of Key Managers:

Name	Title
Henry Smith	VP-Sales
Bob Simpson	Pres.

History/Origins:

Founded by John Smarthoff in 1980. Merged with Data Software in 1985.

Questions to Ask During Interviews:

1. Impact on Co. by current slump in computer
2. sales?
3. what new concepts/software on horizon?
4. How sales group is perceived by tech group –
5. what are relationships like?

what expect of me during 1st year?

My comments that made a positive Impact:

1. my Knowledge of the OS/6
2. my willingness to relocate to San José

Comments that weren't well received:

1. my question about sales vs. tech groups
2. my interest in fast advancement

Names of people I met:

Name	Title
Marge Hollins	Reg. Sales Mgr.
Tim Teagarten	Tech Service Mgr.
Robert Hewitt	Asst HR Mgr.

Items to follow through on:

Items	Date for Action
1. Call to set up appt with Mr Smith	2 / 10 / 9–
2. Contact Mike about stressing in	/ /
3. the reference check my	/ /
4. good closing skills	2 / 9 / 9–

SKILL BUILDER 3

Company Fact Sheet

— Preparing for your Interview —

Company Name: ______________________

Location: ______________________

Contacts: ***(People I know who work there or know the Company)***

Name: ____________ Name: ____________

Tel #: ____________ Tel #: ____________

Kind of Business: ***(Products and/or Services)***

____

Names of Some Typical Customers:

____________ ____________ ____________

____________ ____________ ____________

Significant Facts:

Annual Sales Volume: $ ______________________

Growth Pattern (past 5 yrs.) ______________________

____

Number of Employees: ____________ Headqtr. Location: ____________

Other Locations: ____________ ____________ ____________

Interesting Production Statistics: ______________________

____

Names of Key Managers: Name: ____________ Title: ____________

____________ ____________

____________ ____________

History/Origins:

____

____

____

Questions to Ask During Interviews:

1. ______
2. ______
3. ______
4. ______
5. ______

My comments that made a positive Impact:

1. ______
______
2. ______
______

Comments that weren't well received:

1. ______
______
2. ______
______

Names of people I met:

Name: ______ Title: ______

Name: ______ Title: ______

Name: ______ Title: ______

Items to follow through on: **Date for Action**

1. ______ ___/___/___
2. ______ ___/___/___
3. ______ ___/___/___
4. ______ ___/___/___

Company Fact Sheet

— Preparing for your Interview —

Company Name: ______________________

Location: ______________________

Contacts: ***(People I know who work there or know the Company)***

Name: ____________ Name: ____________

Tel #: ____________ Tel #: ____________

Kind of Business: ***(Products and/or Services)***

____

Names of Some Typical Customers:

______ ______ ______

______ ______ ______

Significant Facts:

Annual Sales Volume: $ ______________________

Growth Pattern (past 5 yrs.) ______________________

____

Number of Employees: ____________ Headqtr. Location: ____________

Other Locations: ______ ______ ______

Interesting Production Statistics: ______________________

____

Names of Key Managers: Name: ____________ Title: ____________

____________ ____________

____________ ____________

History/Origins:

____

____

____

Questions to Ask During Interviews:

1. ______________________
2. ______________________
3. ______________________
4. ______________________
5. ______________________

My comments that made a positive Impact:

1. ______________________
____
2. ______________________
____

Comments that weren't well received:

1. ______________________
____
2. ______________________
____

Names of people I met:

Name: ______________ Title: ______________
Name: ______________ Title: ______________
Name: ______________ Title: ______________

Items to follow through on: **Date for Action**

1. ______________________ ____/____/____
2. ______________________ ____/____/____
3. ______________________ ____/____/____
4. ______________________ ____/____/____

Company Fact Sheet

— Preparing for your Interview —

Company Name: ______________________

Location: ______________________

Contacts: ***(People I know who work there or know the Company)***

Name: ____________ Name: ____________

Tel #: ____________ Tel #: ____________

Kind of Business: ***(Products and/or Services)***

____

Names of Some Typical Customers:

____________ ____________ ____________

____________ ____________ ____________

Significant Facts:

Annual Sales Volume: $ ______________________

Growth Pattern (past 5 yrs.) ______________________

____

Number of Employees: ____________ Headqtr. Location: ____________

Other Locations: ____________ ____________ ____________

Interesting Production Statistics: ______________________

____

Names of Key Managers: Name: ____________ Title: ____________

____________ ____________

____________ ____________

History/Origins:

____

____

____

Questions to Ask During Interviews:

1. ______________________________
2. ______________________________
3. ______________________________
4. ______________________________
5. ______________________________

My comments that made a positive Impact:

1. ______________________________
____
2. ______________________________
____

Comments that weren't well received:

1. ______________________________
____
2. ______________________________
____

Names of people I met:

Name: ____________________ Title: ____________________

Name: ____________________ Title: ____________________

Name: ____________________ Title: ____________________

Items to follow through on: **Date for Action**

1. ____________________ ____/____/____
2. ____________________ ____/____/____
3. ____________________ ____/____/____
4. ____________________ ____/____/____

Company Fact Sheet

— Preparing for your Interview —

Company Name: ____________________

Location: ____________________

Contacts: ***(People I know who work there or know the Company)***

Name: ____________ Name: ____________

Tel #: ____________ Tel #: ____________

Kind of Business: ***(Products and/or Services)***

____

Names of Some Typical Customers:

____________ ____________ ____________

____________ ____________ ____________

Significant Facts:

Annual Sales Volume: $ ____________________

Growth Pattern (past 5 yrs.) ____________________

____

Number of Employees: ____________ Headqtr. Location: ____________

Other Locations: ____________ ____________ ____________

Interesting Production Statistics: ____________________

____

Names of Key Managers: Name: ____________ Title: ____________

____________ ____________

____________ ____________

History/Origins:

____

____

____

Questions to Ask During Interviews:

1. ______
2. ______
3. ______
4. ______
5. ______

My comments that made a positive Impact:

1. ______
______
2. ______
______

Comments that weren't well received:

1. ______
______
2. ______
______

Names of people I met:

Name: ______ Title: ______
Name: ______ Title: ______
Name: ______ Title: ______

Items to follow through on: **Date for Action**

1. ______ ___/___/___
2. ______ ___/___/___
3. ______ ___/___/___
4. ______ ___/___/___

Company Fact Sheet

— Preparing for your Interview —

Company Name: ____________________

Location: ____________________

Contacts: ***(People I know who work there or know the Company)***

Name: ____________ Name: ____________

Tel #: ____________ Tel #: ____________

Kind of Business: ***(Products and/or Services)***

____

Names of Some Typical Customers:

____________ ____________ ____________

____________ ____________ ____________

Significant Facts:

Annual Sales Volume: $ ____________________

Growth Pattern (past 5 yrs.) ____________________

____

Number of Employees: ____________ Headqtr. Location: ____________

Other Locations: ____________ ____________ ____________

Interesting Production Statistics: ____________________

____

Names of Key Managers: Name: ____________ Title: ____________

____________ ____________

____________ ____________

History/Origins:

____

____

____

Questions to Ask During Interviews:

1. ______
2. ______
3. ______
4. ______
5. ______

My comments that made a positive Impact:

1. ______
______
2. ______
______

Comments that weren't well received:

1. ______
______
2. ______
______

Names of people I met:

Name: ______ Title: ______
Name: ______ Title: ______
Name: ______ Title: ______

Items to follow through on: **Date for Action**

1. ______ ____/____/____
2. ______ ____/____/____
3. ______ ____/____/____
4. ______ ____/____/____

Company Fact Sheet

— Preparing for your Interview —

Company Name: ______________________

Location: ______________________

Contacts: ***(People I know who work there or know the Company)***

Name: ____________ Name: ____________

Tel #: ____________ Tel #: ____________

Kind of Business: ***(Products and/or Services)***

____

Names of Some Typical Customers:

____________ ____________ ____________

____________ ____________ ____________

Significant Facts:

Annual Sales Volume: $ ______________________

Growth Pattern (past 5 yrs.) ______________________

____

Number of Employees: ____________ Headqtr. Location: ____________

Other Locations: ____________ ____________ ____________

Interesting Production Statistics: ______________________

____

Names of Key Managers: Name: ____________ Title: ____________

____________ ____________

____________ ____________

History/Origins:

____

____

____

Questions to Ask During Interviews:

1. ______________________________
2. ______________________________
3. ______________________________
4. ______________________________
5. ______________________________

My comments that made a positive Impact:

1. ______________________________

____

2. ______________________________

____

Comments that weren't well received:

1. ______________________________

____

2. ______________________________

____

Names of people I met:

Name: ____________________ Title: ____________________

Name: ____________________ Title: ____________________

Name: ____________________ Title: ____________________

Items to follow through on: **Date for Action**

1. ____________________ ____/____/____
2. ____________________ ____/____/____
3. ____________________ ____/____/____
4. ____________________ ____/____/____

Chapter 5

Preparing Your Questions

What do you say when the interviewer asks, "Do you have any questions?"

If your response is, "I can't think of any right now" or, "I don't have any," you are going to make a negative impression; you are likely to come across as someone who is not particularly interested in the position or the organization. It could even appear that you are so desperate for a job that you will take whatever is being offered. Interviewers often use this question to gauge the depth of your motivation to get the job or your prudence in researching the organization. In any case, it is important to plan beforehand some of the questions you will ask, if you have the opportunity.

Good questions can greatly enhance the impact you make. They also help you determine whether or not the job is a good match for you.

The Best Frame of Mind for Asking Questions

In approaching your interviews, remember that most are really two-way streets (although exceptions such as the stress interview do exist). While the interviewer needs to learn about you, to see if you're qualified, you need to determine if the job meets your needs. It is normal and expected that you'll want to learn all you can about what the job opportunities are.

I therefore recommend that you enter into each interview situation with the understanding that you are there to determine whether or not the job is right for you. If it is, you will try to sell yourself in order to get it. Of course, this last comment is a bit idealistic, since you may have to gain favor with the interviewer before you even get a chance to ask questions. Nonetheless, entering the interview with the awareness that both you and the interviewer are meeting so that you can learn from each other can be very helpful. It can often reduce some of the anxiety many applicants experience when they begin an interview—especially if they perceive the situation as one in which they alone are the targets of questions.

The Right Questions to Ask

Generally speaking, the best questions to ask are those that:

- Help you determine if this is the job you want
- Make a positive impact on the interviewer
- Provide insights into what you should highlight about your background and qualifications

Questions that meet these criteria usually concern:

- What the job is like
- What the company is looking for in a candidate
- How you will fit in
- What is going on in the company

Some of the best questions to ask can be derived from the information you have listed on your Company Fact Sheet. An example of such a question is:

> "I have read that ______________ was happening here in the company. Do you expect this to continue, or is a change expected in the near future?"

If, for some reason, you have not picked up on current trends in the company, you can use a few all-purpose questions, which are usually well-received.

All-Purpose Questions

> "Whether I fill this job or not, can you tell me what your expectations are for the incumbent in this position?"*

> "What do you see for this company in the future—particularly as it might impact on career opportunities?"

> "What would I be expected to accomplish in the job we are discussing?"*

> "What opportunities for advancement are typically available to people in this position?"

*Note: If you can weave these questions into an early segment of the interview, chances are you will learn what is important to the interviewer; you can then tailor your presentation accordingly.

"Can you tell me why this position is vacant?"

"How does this position fit into the organizational structure?"

"How would you describe the management philosophy of this company?"

"What are this department's most important current projects?"

"How much autonomy would I have in this job?"

"How many subordinates would be under my direct supervision? Can you tell me something about these people?"

"Will you please tell me about the person I would report to and other key people I would be dealing with?"

What *Not* to Ask About

What you refrain from asking an interviewer can influence the impression you make as much as what you do ask. In general, discretion in asking about compensation and fringe benefits is called for.

Benefits and Retirement Options

It is usually *not* good strategy to ask about benefits or retirement in an initial interview. Unless these aspects of your employment are critical to your decision about taking the job, save these questions for a discussion *after* the offer is made. Interviewers often interpret an applicant's focus on fringe items or retirement benefits as suggesting an undue concern with security and/or a lack of real interest in job challenges or opportunities.

The Question About Money

There are very few jobs in which salary or compensation is not of primary concern. As an applicant, you need to know what the organization expects to pay you. This is not an item about which you need to decide whether or not to ask; it is more a matter of *when* to ask it.

The appropriate timing of the "what will I be paid?" question often depends on the job level. For most nonexempt jobs, the hourly rate or wage is usually mentioned by the interviewer right up front. Often you will know what the rate is before the interview begins. If you don't know the rate and the interviewer doesn't tell you, it would be quite appropriate to bring up the question of compensation at a point fairly late in the interview. Say, for example, you are applying for a secretarial position. If, during the first fifteen to twenty minutes of the interview, nothing is said about how much you'll be paid, it would be fitting to say (at a judicious point):

> "Before we get much further into discussing me or the job, could you please tell me what my salary would be?"

In fact, for most hourly jobs, if the employer avoids mentioning the salary, it is quite likely that the rate is not particularly attractive.

For exempt positions—especially professional and managerial—it is risky to bring up compensation issues early in the interview process. Premature inquiries about money matters often lead interviewers to conclude that "all he cares about is money." Of course, everyone, including the interviewer, knows that money is important. But in most cases, interviewers trying to fill upper-level positions are ostensibly looking for people who are more concerned about the nature of the challenges, how they can contribute, the company's growth, and the future than about how much they will be paid. It is almost always bad judgment to initiate compensation questions except for the following reasons:

- The interviewer opens the door to the topic, for instance, by asking, "What are your compensation needs?"
- An offer has already been extended.
- The interview is nearing its conclusion (and compensation matters have not been discussed).

For a more complete discussion of salary negotiations, see Chapter 19 on negotiating.

Your Questions and Multiple Interviewers: What to Do

In most organizations it is very likely that you will be interviewed by several different individuals—a representative of the human resources department, one or more operating managers, and perhaps members of the support staff. I discuss how to handle these different interviews in Chapters 12 and 13. Right now, the importance of discussing multiple interviewers is that all of them may ask, "Do you have any questions?"

The temptation will be to ask fewer and fewer questions as you progress from one interviewer to the next. It is critical to resist this temptation.

Each interviewer will be judging you independently, so the kinds of questions you ask have a definite bearing on the impression you make. Also, you may find that the answers you receive to the same questions are not consistent from interviewer to interviewer. If the issue is important to you, ask for clarification during one of the subsequent interviews. Be careful not to question the integrity of any interviewer, but simply express your dilemma. You might say, for instance:

> "I'm a little puzzled. When I asked that same question of Mrs. Jones, she said ________________. and now you say ________________. Can you please clarify the situation for me?"

I recommend that you prepare three to five meaningful questions. Ask at least three of them with each interviewer, even though it means repeating them in each interview.

These questions can be written in the spaces provided on the Company Fact Sheet and reviewed just before your interviews.

For now, however, to help you start developing your list of questions, try Skill Builder 4.

SKILL BUILDER 4
Developing Your Questions

Think for a moment what you want or need to know about a job or a company you might work for. Simply let your thoughts flow off the top of your head.

For the moment, don't worry about setting priorities or having each question fully spelled out. In section A below, jot a few words for each question—just enough so that you'll remember what the issue is.

A. What I'd like to know about any job or company I might work for is:

1. (example) *opportunities for advancement*
2. ________________________
3. ________________________
4. ________________________
5. ________________________
6. ________________________

7. ______________________________

8. ______________________________

B. Now, after considering what was said in this chapter about questions to avoid asking (e.g., about retirement), cross out any that might produce a negative reaction from an interviewer.

C. In the space provided, rewrite the remaining items from your list in section A in question form. Write just as you would ask them in a real interview. Select the best four or five. Remember, the most productive questions, from your standpoint, are ones that will tell you:

- What the job is like
- What the company is looking for in a candidate
- How you will fit in
- What is going on in the company

1. ______________________________
____
____

2. ______________________________
____
____

3. ______________________________
____
____

4. ______________________________
____
____

5. ______________________________
____
____

D. Now, turn to the list of all-purpose questions provided earlier in this chapter to see if any of them are important for you to ask. If you haven't already included them, enter them in any empty spaces in section C or in the spaces that follow:

1. ____

____

____

2. ____

____

____

3. ____

When the time for your next interview arrives, review the questions you have developed in sections C and D and select the most appropriate ones; enter them on your Company Fact Sheet. At that time, you may also want to add a question or two that is specifically targeted toward that particular organization.

Chapter 6
How to Answer Your Interviewer's Questions: A Dozen Tough Ones

Anyone who has been interviewed for a job has probably learned that it is difficult to answer certain questions without conveying something negative. One such classic question is, "What are some of your shortcomings?" It is important to anticipate these "sticky wickets" and to rehearse how you will respond to them.

Some Good Ways to Practice Your Responses

An effective way to practice shaping answers to difficult questions is to use a tape recorder. Dictate the question, give the response you think will sound best, and then listen to your answer. Most individuals who are not experienced at interviewing are surprised at the results of their first attempt. The odds are great that your answer will sound weak, confused, or self-damaging. It will probably be quite evident that you need to work on better ways to phrase your answer. A good approach to critiquing your response is to ask yourself, "What would my reaction be if I were the interviewer and heard that response?"

Having a friend (ideally, one who does a fair amount of interviewing) listen to your responses can be most helpful in developing alternative ways of coping with various questions.

Two Basic Types of Tough Questions

There are two basic kinds of questions that present problems for most job applicants. One group consists of questions that require you to talk about or evaluate yourself. An example of such a question is, "What is there about you that would make you an effective supervisor?"

The second type of tough question requests the applicant to solve a problem—real or hypothetical. An example of this line of questioning is, "What do you think is the ideal way to minimize conflicts between sales and manufacturing departments?" Sometimes these questions are phrased in hypothetical terms, such as, "Suppose one of your best subordinates indicates that he wants to leave the company. How would you handle such a situation?"

As I discuss ways of dealing with self-evaluative questions, please be aware that they are limitless in nature. There is simply no way to prepare yourself for *all* that may be asked—especially by experienced, professional interviewers. However, there are some good, general principles that will enable you to formulate effective responses to these difficult questions. These strategies are presented in Chapter 14. For now, though, I will concentrate on some of the more commonly asked difficult questions.

Twelve of the Toughest Questions

The most frequently asked "sticky wickets" are described next, along with suggestions about how to prepare for them. Exactly how you answer them will depend on your background and personality. However, it should be fairly easy to adapt these principles to your own situation.

1. "Tell Me About Yourself."

This is the granddaddy of all self-report questions. For most job applicants, it is also the most difficult one to respond to. If you have not prepared yourself and rehearsed an answer to this question, it is likely that you will come across in an unimpressive way.

For most interviewers, *what* you say in response to this question is not as important as *how* you handle it. The most frequent tendency is to say too much. Applicants usually give too much detail—they bore the interviewer, go off on tangents, or reveal information about themselves that is better left unsaid.

Here is an effective strategy for answering the "tell me about yourself" question. It is called *three steps and a bridge*. It covers four areas:

1. Your early background (e.g., where you were brought up)
2. Your education
3. Your work experience

4. A bridging statement such as, "and that background leads me here today to this assignment."

The idea is to touch *briefly* on each of the first three areas and single out a few significant achievements. You then follow this summary by a bridging phase.

Here is an example of how you might use the three-steps-and-a-bridge method.

> "I was brought up in a suburban area in New Jersey. Both of my parents were schoolteachers, so the idea of getting a good education was instilled in me early on.
>
> In high school, I was quite good at math. My teachers and my parents thought that engineering would be a natural for me. I also liked the science courses, so I also thought that some sort of career in technology would be good.
>
> After graduation, I was accepted at Rutgers University and got a B.S. in mechanical engineering. While there I was an officer in a social fraternity and was elected president of the Junior class. I also did quite well academically, making the Dean's List seven out of the eight semesters.
>
> After Rutgers, I took a job with Allied Chemical, starting in their management training program. After two years, I was assigned to a large plant in Wilmington, Delaware, and soon found myself involved in a major production control problem for which I was able to develop a solution—a computerized program. Soon after, I was moved up to a supervisory position. I found that I enjoyed the managing as much as the engineering.
>
> The management experience led me to pursue an MBA in the evenings. Then, one year later, I was contacted by a headhunter who told me of a unique opportunity at Perkin-Elmer Corporation—they wanted somebody with high-tech production experience and computer know-how. The job attracted me because it gave me a chance to advance in management and also work on the development of new equipment.
>
> I have been at Perkin-Elmer now for three years as assistant manager of technical development, and it's *this combination of engineering experience, computer know-how, and management that leads me here today to the position we are discussing.*"

In almost every instance, you will find that an answer of this sort, which takes only two minutes, makes a positive impression.

Because this is such a common and yet crucial question, it would be well worthwhile to shape your answer before your next interview. To assist you in organizing your thoughts, try Skill Builder 5, at the end of this chapter.

2. *"What Are Your Strengths?"*

This question should be looked upon as a welcome gift. It provides a wonderful opportunity to tell the interviewer about some specific and important attributes that you possess.

In preparing your answer to this question, *mention at least four or five strengths.* This enables you to present a wide range of assets and also to project a good level of self-confidence. If you present fewer than four, it does not say much about your self-image. Figure 6-1 identifies the factors that contribute to success in any career.

It is helpful to be conversant with the four elements listed in the figure, since your answer to the question about your strengths should describe at least one good quality for each factor. Following are descriptions of the four factors and examples of appropriate statements you can make about them.

1. *Intellect.* This factor has nothing to do with knowledge; it relates to capabilities in two dimensions—natural aptitudes (e.g., quantitative, verbal, mechanical, artistic) and how you usually process your thoughts (e.g., think quickly on your feet, think in a logical, deductive manner).

Here are four examples of ways to state your particular intellectual strengths:

> [*Aptitude:*] "One thing about me is that I believe I am fairly bright. I learn very rapidly and can usually pick up on what has to be done in short order."

Figure 6-1. Factors that account for success at work.

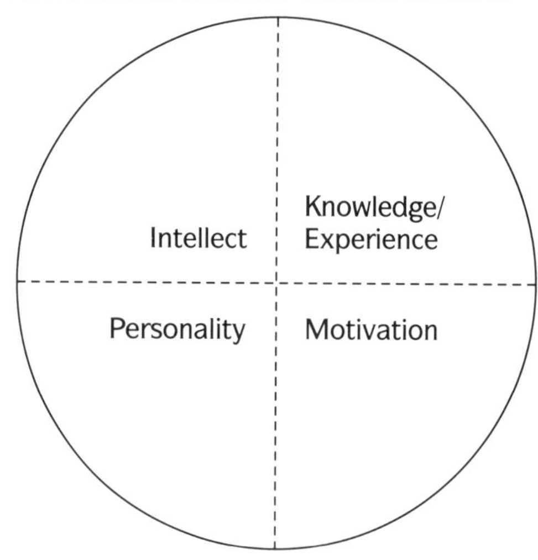

[*Aptitude:*] "I have good quantitative skills—I find it very easy to work with numbers."

[*Process:*] "I am usually quite decisive because I can think quickly on my feet."

[*Aptitude and process:*] "I seem to have good conceptual ability. I usually look at problems from a broad perspective."

2. *Knowledge and Experience.* There is no mystery about this factor. It is just what it sounds like—educational or work achievements that are pertinent to the job for which you are applying. Here are a few examples:

[*Experience:*] "My ten years of sales experience with headquarters buyers should enable me to develop a really effective key accounts campaign."

[*Knowledge:*] "The training I've had in computer sciences should enable me to step in and be productive from day one."

Note how it is helpful to mention the know-how or experience and then relate that to what it could positively mean for the company.

3. *Personality.* This factor has to do with your behavioral characteristics (how you interact with others) and your temperament (how you typically behave). Here are some examples:

[*Skill:*] "I seem to have good ability to relate to people at all levels in the company. I'm interested in others and I think they sense that."

[*Trait and Skill:*] "Another strength I have is that I don't discourage easily. If I run into an obstacle, I'm likely to persist until I find some way around it."

4. *Motivation.* This factor has to do with your interests (activities you enjoy doing), your drive, and your energy level. Here are some examples:

[*Interests:*] "I'm quite extroverted. While I am good at technical problem solving, I really enjoy working with others. I find supervising stimulating and challenging."

or

"I like to pay a lot of attention to the fine points. I don't just skip through a job; I exercise a lot of care and, as a result, I'm accurate."

[*Drive:*] "I've always been a self-starter. I guess I have a lot of drive because I get tremendous satisfaction out of seeing a goal accomplished."

[*Energy:*] "I have a high energy level. I can work long hours without getting tired."

Describing Your Strengths

To help you make the most of this important "strengths" question, it is helpful to write out your assets. Try to develop six and, even more important, *at least one for each of the factors.* As you will see later, this list of attributes will be useful throughout the interview and is an important discussion topic to have down pat.

Completing Skill Builder 6, at the end of the chapter, can assist you in developing this critical list of major strengths.

3. *"What Are Your Major Weaknesses or Limitations?"*

First of all, you should recognize that this question is often phrased in more subtle ways, usually in an effort to make the question appear less threatening to the applicant. Some common ways in which it is stated are:

"What are some areas in which you can improve?"

"How have you grown over the past few years?"

"Where do you see yourself needing to grow in the near future?"

Second, it is not good strategy to attempt to avoid mentioning shortcomings. Unless you are extremely sure of yourself, ducking the shortcomings issue will come across as being defensive, a sign of weakness. On the other hand, you don't have to condemn yourself either. My recommendation is to mention one or two limitations and state them in such a way that they are not damaging to you. There are two basic techniques for accomplishing this:

1. Mention weaknesses that "mirror" your assets.
2. Mention weaknesses that are easily remedied.

Let's begin with the "mirror concept" of presenting your weaknesses.

Many applicants find the "shortcomings" question difficult or awkward to deal with. Actually, it can be comfortable to answer, once a certain principle is understood: *Your weaknesses are almost always overextensions of your strengths.* For instance, if you are action-oriented, the positive side is that you are probably decisive, can juggle many projects at once, and get much accomplished in a short period of time. However, when you overplay your strength, you are likely to be criticized for being impatient, not paying enough attention to detail, and not being well-organized. When you formulate an answer to the "shortcomings" question, simply select one of your strengths and admit that sometimes, *because of the strength,* a particular shortcoming is evident. Here are two examples:

> "I tend to look at problems from a "big picture" point of view, and sometimes I don't pay enough attention to the details."
>
> "I'm a high-energy person and push myself pretty hard. I have to be careful sometimes not to move ahead before my staff is ready."

This strategy is an ideal way to talk about your shortcomings. First of all, it is honest. It will ring true along with the positive things you have said about yourself. Second, when you respond by revealing shortcomings that are an overplay of your strengths, your openness conveys self-assurance. That behavior, in its own right, creates a favorable impression on most interviewers. You are not likely to be evaluated as being defensive.

The second suggestion for responding to the "shortcomings" question is to mention something that is easily remedied. The simplest way to do this is to offer an example from the Knowledge Factor (see Figure 6-1) and then state what you intend to do about it. For instance:

> "I would like to take some formal courses in supervision. So far, I've only had my job experiences along with some reading on my own."
>
> "I'd like to strengthen my knowledge of computer applications in sales."
>
> "I could probably improve my public speaking skills—I'd like to take a Toastmasters or Dale Carnegie course."
>
> "I'd like to broaden my managerial skills. I plan to start working on my MBA by taking evening courses."

Since it is so important to handle this question properly, completing Skill Builder 7 at the end of this chapter will help you prepare a good response to this question about your weaknesses.

4. *"What Are Your Financial Requirements?"*

First of all, let's discuss what not to say. Please do not say, "It's not that important to me—opportunity is my primary concern." Of course "opportunity" is a big element in your employment decisions, but compensation is also very important. Would you accept a new job for $20,000 less than you are making now? Money is important not only for how it allows you to live but for what it says about the importance of the job and its incumbent. The point is that money is usually an important issue, and, as applicant, you are not likely to come across as convincing if you duck the question.

In considering how to answer the money question, two issues need to be weighed:

1. How much do you want?
2. How much will they pay?

While no one can prescribe the right salary for you, some considerations can help you to formulate your answer to this question ahead of time. One question to ask yourself is, "What is the minimum I will accept?" This figure should be an amount below which you will not consider the job, regardless of anything else. It's an amount that will permit you to live on the borderline of the lifestyle you want. Write this amount here:

Minimum income I will accept: $______ (week, month, or year)

A second question to answer for yourself is, "How much do I really want?" Enter that amount here:

How much I really want: $______ (week, month, or year)

Having decided upon the two amounts above, you now have a working range—an *acceptance zone* in which to discuss salary.

This leads us to the next part of the equation: How much is the organization willing to pay? If you already know this (because of an advertised wage or other source), and assuming the stated salary falls into your acceptable zone, you can mention a somewhat higher salary than is being offered. It is always easier to back down to the posted amount than to try to go up, once you have stated a desired salary.

If you do not know the salary the organization has in mind, try to determine its expectations before you mention your desires. Here is the one way of getting at that number:

When the interviewer asks you about your salary requirements, you can respond by asking a question of your own:

> "I'd like to answer that question, but would you mind sharing with me the salary grade range for this job?"

If the interviewer states the range, it is usually prudent to select a figure that is halfway between the midpoint and the top of the salary range. You may have to back down to the midpoint, but if you mention a number below that amount, you have given away any negotiating strength.

If the interviewer is unwilling to talk about the grade range or the salary figure she has in mind, one acceptable option is to mention an amount equal to your current salary plus 15 percent. If you state your desired salary at the amount you are now making, it does not say much to the interviewer about your ambition or sense of self-worth.

Of course, everything I've said so far is designed to fit the typical employment situation. How much compensation you ask for really depends on how much you believe you are worth. There are times when it may be quite appropriate to ask for two or three times your current earnings. The determining factor is how much your prospective employer believes you are worth.

The main point about answering the "how much" question is not stumbling for an answer or seeming embarrassed about your response. Before you go to the interview, know your acceptance zone and state your financial desires firmly and confidently.

For a more detailed discussion of the strategies of salary negotiations, see Section Four, which discusses what you do after the interview.

5. *"Why [Are You Leaving/Did You Leave] Your Present Position?"*

In asking this question, the interviewer is looking to discover whether or not you were terminated, "eased out," or quit because things were not going well for you on the job. More specifically, she is concerned about your ability to get along with people. The interviewer will be listening very carefully to your wording, seeking to pick up negative attitudes toward your co-workers or bosses.

In responding to this question, it is best to answer truthfully, but in a way that is not self-damaging. Sometimes the actual situation provides a perfectly acceptable explanation. You might, for instance, have left the position because the company was losing money and the future held little potential for growth. Or your company may have been taken over in an acquisition, and your department was eliminated.

In the 1990s, organization downsizing will continue to be commonplace. If you were part of a major corporate reduction in force (RIF), you might as well be up-front about it. These days RIFs are so much a part of the corporate world that your interviewer isn't likely to judge you negatively because a downsizing has you in the job marketplace. However, *how* you answer is important. No hint of defensiveness should be conveyed. Make your answer brief and matter of fact. For instance:

Situation: Fired Because of a Major Downsizing

[*Bad:*] "As you know, the company has been experiencing difficulty in the past several years, and they've gradually had to reduce staff. But last month, things really got serious and. . . ."

[*Good:*] "Last month the company had a major downsizing, and like most of the technical staff, I got caught in it."

If you left because you were fired, it is critical to carefully rehearse how you answer this question. Many applicants will come across better by being open and frank about being fired than by trying to duck what actually happened. However, if you talk about being fired, it is most important not to imply your termination was caused by low motivation or inability to work effectively with others. Notice, in the examples below, how a negative is positively positioned:

Situation: Fired Because of a Conflict With Boss

[*Bad:*] "My boss and I didn't get along that well."

[*Good:*] "To be perfectly frank with you, I got fired. My boss and I had completely different management styles. We both respected each other, so over the years we had more or less agreed to disagree. But, eventually he wanted more things done his way than I was willing to do."

Situation: Performance Was Not What Boss Wanted

[*Bad:*] "Even though I was doing everything she wanted, I just couldn't do enough to please my boss."

[*Good:*] "The job really didn't let me capitalize on my best talents. I have good ability to supervise and motivate others, but I was mostly tied up with backroom technical assignments."

To help you work on this very importance response, a worksheet is provided in Skill Builder 8.

6. "What Are Your Career Goals for the Next Five Years?"

Usually the interviewer asks this question to determine (1) your drive and ambition, and (2) if your expectations for advancement match what the company can offer.

About Your Drive and Ambition

Even if you are uncertain about your future, it is important to articulate a general desire for continued growth. If you indicate that you have no career goals, the interviewer will almost always interpret that response negatively.

> [*Not:*] "I don't have any particular goals for the next five years. I like to look at opportunities as they come."

> [*Rather:*] "I like to have the feeling that I am continually growing, so in the next five years I want to increase my competence in ______________."

On the other hand, being too ambitious is also risky.

> [*Poor:*] "My goal is to become a top executive in this company. I expect that with my drive I'll move ahead very rapidly."

The part about becoming a "top executive" is okay, but once you add the words "very rapidly" you sound like someone whose ambition overrides everything else. Some interviewers may even be feel threatened by such a comment.

In today's "flat" organizations, rapid advancement is not typical. It is best to strike a balance: Show desire for progress and growth, but be realistic considering the job level and the organization.

If you have specific career objectives, it usually is helpful to state them. The risk, however, is that they might be incompatible with the company's view of your potential or the opportunities available. If you know enough about the organization, you can often judge how closely your goals match the company's expectations. When they are fairly congruent, you can state your goals succinctly and confidently. For example:

> "Within the next two years I would like to advance to the level of sales supervisor so that at the end of four or five years I would be ready for promotion to district sales manager."

Your Goals vs. Organization Goals

When you are uncertain about the match between your goals and those of the organization, it is prudent to hedge a bit until you can learn more about future possibilities in the company. You might state it like this:

> "Within the next five years I want to expand my professional selling skills and advance into sales management—but I'd need to know a

little more about your organization to tell you exactly what level or when."

An opportunity is provided for you to work on your response to the "goals" question in Skill Builder 9.

7. "What Kind of a Position Are You Looking For?"

This question, much like "tell me about yourself," can be difficult because it is easy to say too much or the wrong thing. From the interviewer's standpoint, there is concern that what you want is different from the job the company is trying to fill. It may be looking for a secretary; you are seeking a position as office manager. It is looking for someone to travel a lot; you want more regular hours and schedule.

Try to answer this one concisely, viewing it as an opportunity to highlight your strengths. It is usually safer, too, to avoid using specific job titles unless you have applied for a specific position. Here are some examples of phrases that illustrate the point:

- I am looking for work where I can apply my skills with people [*mention here those specific skills or activities you enjoy*].
- I am looking for a job in which I can use my good technical skills [*mention here what they are*].
- I am looking for an opportunity that allows me to use my skill with [*things/machines/tools*].

In summary, until you can learn more about what the company is actually looking for, it is best to mention a few positive attributes; at the same time, keep your answer sufficiently generic to avoid eliminating yourself from further consideration.

Of course, there are exceptions to what has just been said. If you are seeking a specific position or job level, then state your goal firmly and confidently. When applicants speak of a definite career preference, it usually comes across positively, conveying self-assurance and a strong sense of self-worth.

Even if what the organization has to offer is different from the job you said you wanted, the interviewer may be so impressed with your confidence that he tells you about the job they are trying to fill. He may even try to convince you that it would be a good choice. Listen carefully; it might be!

Skill Builder 10 provides an opportunity for you to develop an effective answer to questions concerning job preferences.

8. *"What Was Your Most Significant Accomplishment in Your Last Position?"*

This question represents another excellent opportunity to describe your capabilities. However, it requires some thought and preparation. Sophisticated interviewers will be attempting to determine the true significance of your role in the accomplishment. Experience has taught them that applicants often describe important projects in which they played a part but which they did not actually propose, create, design, or manage. The interviewer will be seeking to determine if a consultant or someone else actually shepherded the project.

To best answer this question, you need to think of an achievement that was clearly "your baby" and that had a positive impact. It also will help if you can describe obstacles that needed to be overcome (such as initial resistance to your project or difficulties that were surmounted along the way). Here is an example:

> "Last year, even though the company reorganized and I lost four salespeople, I was able, through extensive 'hands-on' training of the remaining sales force, to increase sales in my district by 42 percent."

Following the steps outlined in Skill Builder 11 will enable you to prepare the perfect answer to this question.

9. *"Doesn't This Job Represent a Step Down From the Level of Work You've Been Doing?"*

This is a likely question if the job for which you are being interviewed is at a lower level of responsibility or salary than your last position. The interviewer will be concerned that you are only taking this job as a stopgap measure and that you are likely to leave as soon as something better comes along. As applicant, your job will be to convince the interviewer that, if hired, you will make a commitment to the job. Examples of helpful comments are:

> "I like very much what I have learned about this job, and, as with every job I've taken, I'll give it my best.
>
> "In every job situation I think employers worry about people leaving, just as employees worry about getting terminated. I'll do a good job for you and stay just as long as we both agree that this is what I should be doing."

If there is a possibility that your interviewers might challenge your readiness for a particular job, now is the best time to determine how you will respond. Skill Builder 12 can help you handle this question successfully.

10. "How Would You Describe Your [Management Style/ Supervisory Approach]?"

Your response to this question can result in your looking bad, particularly if you seem hesitant or falter in your description. After all, the interviewer expects that if you supervise others a particular way, you should be able to explain it easily. If you can't, it casts some doubt on your ability and experience as a manager.

This question can sometimes be difficult if you're not sure of the prevailing style in the interviewer's organization. Hopefully, however, you will have gleaned some insights about this issue from your research on the company.

There are three basic ways to answer this question, depending upon how hungry you are for the position—

1. *Be brutally honest.* If you have a definite way of managing and you can spell it out clearly and confidently, great. The upside is that you'll sound as if you know what you're doing and have been successful with your approach. The downside is that what you say may be incompatible with the way the organization works. However, the risk is likely to be fairly minimal unless your management style is highly unusual (e.g., "I make all the decisions.").

2. *Key your style to that of the organization.* Some companies have a definite personality that translates into a management pattern. These organizations are often proud of their style and clearly look for the kind of people who will fit in. One client of mine (vice-president of marketing in a Fortune 500 company) often told me that "if the applicant can't take a lot of heat, he won't make it in our business."

This company's management style could be characterized as one of "sink or swim." You can easily see how an applicant might quickly fall into disfavor if she mentioned that she "cared a lot about her people" and put training and development high on her list of priorities.

If you know how management functions, you can mention how certain aspects of your approach to management dovetail with the company's. This represents a low-risk response. Be prepared to give an example or two illustrating your successful application of the company's management style. For example:

> "I am inclined to be demanding of my staff, but participative. I spell out to them what I expect, listen carefully to their reactions, and, once we're in agreement, I give them lots of rope. They know I'm there if

they have a serious problem, but they also know I expect the results we agreed on, at the time we agreed to."

3. *Play it safe.* If you are uncertain of the company's corporate style, you can present a very acceptable answer by mentioning one of several management approaches that are currently seen as effective. Pick one, however, that comes close to describing your actual behavior. Here are a few examples:

> "I like to operate in a participative way. Whenever possible I get commitment from my staff by involving them in the planning and objective setting."
>
> "I have a lot of respect for my staff. I usually give them plenty of rope but clearly hold them accountable. I like to have time to work on ways to improve the bottom line, so I delegate quite freely."

It is important to be able to give your answer clearly and concisely on this question. See Skill Builder 13 for guidance in shaping your answer.

11. "Describe a Time You Failed."

When answering this question, you won't create a positive impression by responding with a comment like, "My job isn't an easy one, but over the years I must have been fortunate. I can't think of any significant failure I've had." The interviewer is likely to interpret this answer as ducking the truth or to conclude that you never took any risks.

This question, as with the other "shortcomings" questions, should be viewed as an opportunity, as a chance to communicate your strengths while you explain how you coped with the failure.

The key to successfully answering this question is to be honest about a failure and then turn the lemon into lemonade. You do this by showing how you profited from the failure or how your talents helped you to overcome it. The generic scenario goes like this: You fell off your bike, dusted yourself off, got back on again, learned that you have to maintain a certain minimal speed, and then rode away.

In brief, present the failure as a positive event by showing how the failure:

- Was a constructive learning experience, i.e., you grew from it.
- Helped you acquire new skills or knowledge.
- Revealed strengths you had not previously been aware of. For example: "Helped me see that I have a lot of inner strength—I don't give up readily and I'm not easily discouraged."

You can prepare yourself for this question by completing Skill Builder 14.

12. "How Would You Approach This Job?"

"Suppose you came on board tomorrow, what is the first thing you would do?" Or, "What actions would you take during your first week [or month] on the job?" These are frequently asked variations of the same basic question.

Interviewers often use these questions when the job for which you are applying involves a "sticky" or sensitive situation. For instance, you may be applying for a managerial job in a department that has recently been downsized; morale is low and everyone is concerned that the ax may fall soon again. The interviewer wants a sense of how you are likely to proceed and of the impact your actions will have on the department staff.

You may be thinking, "That's unfair. How can I answer a question about what I would do if I don't know exactly what is going on?" Precisely. This question is loaded with risk. To minimize the danger, you don't answer immediately; you try to gain more insight into the job setting by asking a question of your own. You attempt to gain a sense of what the interviewer is looking for.

You might say, for instance, "I'd be happy to answer that question, but it would help if I had a better understanding of exactly what the current situation is like. Can you fill me in a bit?"

Responding with a question rather than giving a direct answer will be inappropriate if the job setting has already been discussed or the situation is obvious. In these instances, a few general principles can help you formulate an acceptable answer:

1. *Recognize that, once you are on the job, you will need to survey the new world you've stepped into.* Indicate that you will initially spend time gathering information (from subordinates, sales staff, boss, whoever) in order to learn "firsthand" what needs to be done.

2. *Try to visualize yourself in the assignment.* What do you believe are the probable major issues to be dealt with? You can say, "I imagine that one issue would be . . ." and look to the interviewer for signs of affirmation or rejection. The interviewer's body language may provide a clue as to whether or not you're on the right track.

3. Don't try to explain how you would *solve* a major problem. Instead, mention a few *first steps* you would take to start the ball rolling.

Having said all this, I realize that the question can still be a killer if you say the wrong thing. In the final analysis, it's best to rely on your past experiences and stay with actions and decisions that you have learned work for you.

SKILL BUILDER 5
Shaping Answers to the Invitation: "Tell Me About Yourself"

Remember the strategy for your answer: three steps and a bridge.

For this exercise I suggest that, using the guideline provided, you organize your response to this tough question by writing it out.

STEP 1. Very briefly discuss your early background:

Where were you brought up? ______________________________

____

Any interesting and relevant facts about parents/family? (If not, omit comments): ______________________________

____

____

STEP 2. Describe your education:

If you are a college graduate or have an advanced degree, skip high school, or only mention elements of high school that are relevant to your career choice or current job. For example, "I was good at math and my teachers thought that engineering would be a 'natural' for me." If you are not a college graduate, select only those aspects of high school that reveal outstanding strengths, such as writing or leadership skills.

High school: ______________________________

____

____

College/graduate school: ____

____

____

STEP 3. Discuss your work experience:

Mention only job title, company, and one or two significant achievements. Very briefly explain the reason for any changes in employer (if reason is a positive one, e.g., "was recruited away by another firm"). If you have a long work history, you don't need to mention more than the job title for the early, less important positions.

If you are going for your first full-time job, name any part-time positions that will help you bring in a skill or experience that might be meaningful for the job(s) for which you are applying.

First job: ____

____

____

I left because: ____

Second job: ____

____

____

I left because: ____

Third job: ____

____

____

I left because: ____

Fourth job: ____

____

____

I left because: ____

End your review with the statement, ". . . and this combination of [job exepriences/education/personal traits/skills] leads me here today to the position we are discussing."

Read back over your notations and see what could be eliminated to make your statement more concise. Remember, the interviewer can always ask more questions.

Next, rehearse your answer to the question by saying it out loud and timing it. If it takes more than two minutes, prune it further. You will then be ready for this tough question.

SKILL BUILDER 6
Cataloging Your Strengths

In the spaces below, list two or three strengths *in each* of the four areas of functioning described in Figure 6-1: Intellect, Knowledge and Experience, Personality, and Motivation. Since you won't know which of these areas is most important to your interviewer, it's important to include a strength in each.

INTELLECT FACTOR [natural aptitudes (e.g., ''words come easily to me'') and/or how you think (e.g., ''I can think quickly on my feet.'')]:

1. ______________________________

____

2. ______________________________

____

3. ______________________________

____

KNOWLEDGE/EXPERIENCE FACTOR [strong know-how (e.g., ''I can estimate materials from blueprints'') or exceptional experience (e.g., ''I've had ten years of increasingly responsible sales management experience.'')]:

1. ______________________________

____

2. ______________________________

____

PERSONALITY FACTOR [interpersonal skills (e.g., ''I'm not afraid to step in and take charge'') and/or helpful behavior (e.g., ''I find that I can get quick acceptance from people at all levels in the organization.'')]:

1. ______________________________

____

2. ______________________________

____

MOTIVATION FACTOR [interests (e.g., ''I like jobs that keep me active and on the go''); drive (e.g., ''My goal is to be a district manager in the next two years''); energy level (e.g., ''I can work long hours without getting tired.'')]:

1. ______________________________

____

2. ______________________________

____

Do you feel good about yourself after having put so many positive attributes down on paper? These qualities should be conveyed to your interviewers; describing them is the best way to help interviewers know you and your capabilities. Seek every opportunity to work your strengths into your interview.

If you listed six or more attributes, now go back and circle the four or five that you believe will have the most positive impact. Make sure that you have one for each factor. In this way you can be certain that whatever area is important to the interviewer will be included when you describe your positive attributes.

SKILL BUILDER 7
Answering the "Shortcomings" Question

What will you say in response to the question about your limitations? Developing a good answer takes some practice. In the spaces below, write out how you intend to answer this question.

SHORTCOMING 1: ______________________________

How will I phrase it? (Remember to state the "upside" of the weakness first.) ______________________________

____

____

____

Now, read it over. Does your statement—

a. Suggest that the limitation is simply an overextension of a strength?
b. Sound like something that can easily be corrected or changed?

You should be able to answer yes to either a or b. If you cannot, then you need to revise your answer.

Since it is good practice to have a second shortcoming ready in case your interviewer presses you, write down one more.

SHORTCOMING 2: ______________________________

How will I phrase it? ______________________________

____

____

Does it fulfill either criterion a or b?

If you rehearse giving these answers out loud, you'll be ready for this question during your next interview.

SKILL BUILDER 8
Explaining Why You Left Your Last Job

In the following space, write out your answer to the question, "Why did you leave your last job?" Try to phrase it truthfully, but, at the same time, have it reflect favorably on you.

For example: "I left my last job because of a major reorganization; my job was just eliminated. It has now given me the chance to make a career change I've been thinking about for years: to get out of staff and into line management—into a job just like the one we're talking about here."

Now reflect on your current situation and, as truthfully as possible, write out why you left and how leaving has benefited you.

"I left my last job because ________________________________

________." *Then show how this action was something positive:* "________

____."

This is an important statement to try out to see if it sounds as positive and convincing as you would like it to be. Try giving the explanation to some friends and/or dictate it on a cassette and listen critically to it.

Once you've tried out your statement, it is very likely that some revisions will be in order. In fact, it may take several revisions before it is ready to go. Here are two more spaces in which to write out your revisions.

[*Revision 1:*] "I left my last job because ____________________

____

____

____

____."

[*Revision 2:*] "I left my last job because ____________________

____

____

____

____."

SKILL BUILDER 9
Answering the "Goals" Question

To prepare to answer the "goals" question, write out your career objectives, stating where you would really like to be in five years' time. (It is not necessary to have three):

Career objective 1: ____

____

______________________________. To be achieved by: / / .

Career objective 2: ____

____

______________________________. To be achieved by: / / .

Career objective 3: ____

____

______________________________. To be achieved by: / / .

Now, try to synthesize your goals so that you can explain in a few sentences where you hope to be, careerwise, in five years.

"Within the next five years I hope to ______________________________

____

____

____."

How does it sound? 1) Does it show a desire for progress and growth without seeming overly ambitious? 2) Do your stated ambitions tie in with the kinds of jobs you'll be interviewing for?

Next, revise—especially if you did not give a strong "yes" to questions 1 and 2. ______________________________

____

____

____

____

Can you make this statement with a feeling of confidence and self-assurance? If so, you're ready. Go with it! But if you feel uncomfortable or believe that it won't ring true, another revision is in order.

Try it again here:

"Within the next five years I hope to ______________________________

____

____

______________________________."

SKILL BUILDER 10
Developing Your Job Preference Statement

On the following lines, write what you will say if an interviewer asks, "What kind of position are you looking for?"

____

____

____

____

Check it over. Is your statement:

1. Brief and to the point?
2. Conveying a skill and/or abilities you have?
3. One that sounds as if you know what you want (not wishy-washy)?

If your answer is yes to each of the three questions, then try the statement out on a friend and/or make a tape recording to see how it sounds. If the statement passes this last test, give it a try in your next interview.

If you answered no to any one of the three questions, then try a rewrite in the space below, keeping in mind the three principles. Then give it the same test as suggested for your first pass at this question.

"I am looking for a position that ______________________________

____

____

____

____."

Again, read over your statement. How does it sound? Practical? Mature? Consistent? Try it out on a few friends, and listen to their reactions. If you all agree it sounds good, go with it!

SKILL BUILDER 11
Developing Your Greatest Accomplishment

To handle this question successfully, you need a response that clearly describes the accomplishment itself and includes any hurdles you had to overcome to achieve it. Your response must also be plausible; the achievement must be demonstrably of your own doing.

STEP 1. Get the key facts organized.

"The most significant accomplishment in my last position was to [*describe end results*] ______________________________

______________________________."

"What made it important was [*describe impact of results*] ________

____

______________________________."

"Specific actions [*created/designed/sold*] I took that illustrate my capabilities were ______________________________

____

____

______________________________."

STEP 2. Write a brief statement that you can make during an interview. (Combine all the elements of Step 1 in a simple paragraph.)

____

____

____

____

____

If your explanation of the significant accomplishments requires more space than is provided here, it is probably too long. It should be concise and to the point. If your interviewers want more detail, they will ask more questions.

SKILL BUILDER 12
Response to the Challenge of Being Overqualified

The primary concern of the interviewer is that you will be poorly motivated (because you're not sufficiently challenged) or that you will leave when a higher-level job opportunity comes along. Your answer needs to strongly address these issues.

One effective response is to make a positive comment about your general motivation level. For example: "I have always been a hard-driving person. I have to be achieving, so whatever job I take on, I work hard at it."

Write down one or two of your positive motivational characteristics:

1. ______________________________

2. ______________________________

Now, try to write a brief paragraph about your motivation that will defuse your interviewer's concern about how hard you will apply yourself.

"______________________________

____

______________________________."

Instead of raising the "motivation issue," your interviewer may express concern about your willingness to stay with the job. Some factors that might support your willingness to stick with the job are:

- The fact that you like this kind of work—the job matches your interests.
- You have strong family ties in this location.
- You have confidence in your abilities, and believe that eventually you will be promoted.
- If you make a commitment to a company, you honor it.

In the following space, list those the elements in yourself and your surroundings that represent strong reasons for staying with a job.

1. ______________________________
2. ______________________________
3. ______________________________
4. ______________________________

Now select one or two of these factors and write a paragraph response for your interviewer.

"______________________________

____

____

____

______________________________."

Before leaving this question, read your response aloud. Does it in any way sound defensive? If so, can you revise it so that your statement has a more positive impact?

[*Revision of statement:*] "______________________________

____

____

____

____

______________________________."

SKILL BUILDER 13
Describing Your Management Style

One of the best ways to describe your management style is first to provide a simple overview of the style and then an example or two of your application of it. For instance, here is one taken from the text:

[*Overview:*]: ''I like to operate in a participative way. [*Application example:*] Whenever possible, I get commitment from my staff by involving them in the planning and objective setting.''

In the spaces given, write out your responses to the management style question. Try to keep your answers clear and concise.

1. *Your brutally honest answer:* How do you manage? Find a word that conceptualizes your approach (e.g., participative, decisive, empowering) and then give an example or two of that style in action:

''I manage in a ______________________ style. I like

____

____

____.''

Now, read over your statement. How does it sound? Practical? Mature? Consistent? Try it out on a few friends, and listen to their reactions. If you all agree it sounds good, go with it!

2. *If you know the company:* If you have some information about the company's preferred management style, then it is prudent to reflect those elements of your management style that match those of the organization:

[*Company 1:*] ''I manage in a ________________ style. I like to

____

____

____

____.''

[*Company 2:*] "I manage in a ______________________ style. I like to

____

____

____

____."

Read over your statement. How does it sound? Practical? Mature? Consistent? Try it out on a few friends, and listen to their reactions. If you all agree it sounds good, go with it!

3. *Playing it safe:* If you are uncertain about the organization's management style or if your "brutally honest" description does not sound good, then develop your statement from what you know about generally acceptable management methods. Here are a few concepts that are currently okay to mention: *participative, results-oriented, team-builder.*

   Add examples of your application of the concept.

"I manage in a ______________________________ style. I like to

____

____

____

____."

Again, read over your statement. How does it sound? Practical? Mature? Consistent? Try it out on a few friends, and listen to their reactions. If you all agree it sounds good, go with it!

SKILL BUILDER 14
Discussing Failures

Failures are best discussed by being up-front about the failure and then showing how you eventually overcame the difficulty or profited from it.

The steps below will help you organize an effective response when your interviewer asks you to ''describe a failure.''

STEP 1. Select a failed task that was reasonably significant but not too disastrous:

____

____

____

____

STEP 2. Describe your failure within a broad context of success. For example: ''One of the reasons for my career growth is that I am almost always able to get others to cooperate and pitch in on projects. There was a time, however, when my usual efforts didn't seem to work. . . .'' In this space, describe your failure as an anomaly within a pattern of success:

____

____

____

____

____

STEP 3. Consider next the positive side of the failure. How did you benefit? Did you learn from it? Grow from it? Did the failure lead to a good result later on?

____

____

____

____

____

STEP 4. Assemble your answer now in a short paragraph or two.

"While I have been quite good at ______________, one time I failed was when I ____."

The up-side of it was that ____."

Chapter 7
Your Visual Impact: Looking Right

The first impression you make on the interviewer is likely to have a strong impact on how the interview proceeds as well as on the interviewer's final conclusion about your suitability. Make no mistake about it: *It is vital to make a positive initial impression.* That impact is largely governed by how you look to the interviewer; therefore, effort spent on grooming and dressing appropriately has a very definite payoff.

Principles for Making a Positive Impression

1. *Dress in harmony with the way that those interviewing you are likely to dress.* If you are applying to a manufacturing job where the typical dress is a sport jacket without a tie, wearing a pin-striped business suit is not appropriate. Conversely, the sport jacket is out of place when applying to a bank or financial investment firm. A good rule of thumb is to wear clothing just a little more dressy than that required for everyday use on the job. If you would typically wear blue jeans on the job, consider interviewing in neat slacks with a shirt and sweater.

In general, interviewers are more likely to perceive you as being "one of them" to the extent that you are dressed in the manner of company employees. If you are uncertain about your potential employer's dress style, visit the company location some morning as employees are arriving for work. Note, for example, the colors, clothing style, and accessories.

2. *Do not wear something so striking that attention is drawn to your clothes rather than you.* This almost always means conservative, traditional, and conventional clothing. Clothing that is faddish or has exceptionally bold patterns or colors attracts attention—unfortunately, away from you. Specific suggestions for men and women will be presented later in this chapter.

3. *Pay careful attention to details.* Small annoyances often result in strong negative reactions by interviewers—perhaps unfairly so. Unshined shoes, messy hair, jangling jewelry, mismatched clothing (uncoordinated socks and trousers, clashing blouse and skirt), overly prominent accessories, or untrimmed nails can be interpreted as flaws in your character with a resulting turn-down from the interviewer. I know one executive whose favorite statement about evaluating applicants is, "All I have to do is look at somebody's shoes and I can tell you everything I need to know about them." You may say, "Ridiculous," but rightly or wrongly, that is what this successful executive believes. There are plenty more like him, each with his or her own idiosyncrasies.

4. *Purchase an outfit of high quality that you know looks good on you.* This may mean buying an expensive new suit or dress, but this kind of purchase is a worthwhile investment. Not only will you make a good appearance but with good-looking clothes, you will probably experience an increase in self-confidence. When you know you look good, you are likely to feel good about yourself.

When you are buying that suit or dress, consider getting all the appropriate accessories at the same time. This usually is the most effective way of producing a coordinated, impressive appearance—shirt, tie, shoes, and socks that all match; dress, blouse, hosiery, accessories that harmonize and give a strong sense of being integrated.

If you feel uncertain about how to put your outfit together, make your purchases at a good shop with experienced salespeople. Stores that sell top-quality clothing usually have someone on hand who is good at coordinating a conservative business outfit. It could be a fun experience.

5. *If the interviews take place over more than one day, wear a different outfit each day.* If, for some reason, wearing a different suit or dress each day is not feasible, then at a minimum put on a fresh shirt and different tie; women can benefit from wearing a fresh blouse and different accessories.

6. *Do not go directly from the plane to the interview.* If you have to travel some distance for the interview, the ideal way is to fly in the night before. This provides time for clothes to be hung and the wrinkles to smooth out. It also makes it possible, if necessary, to have clothing freshly pressed at the hotel.

If it is not feasible to arrive at the location the night before, visit the restroom at the interviewing site *before* going into the interview. Check clothes, shoes, hair, makeup; brush off any dandruff. In short, look as well-groomed as possible.

7. *Do not wear anything that connects you with a religious group, political cause, association, or school.* This precaution is simply a matter of minimizing risks. There are more biases out there than there are interviewers who

share your beliefs and preferences. Avoid wearing such items as school rings, political buttons, religious symbols, or ties with logos on them.

8. *Do use breath mints.* This is a matter of being safe rather than sorry. Not only is there the obvious problem of the odor of food, but very often anxiety can result in bad breath. Popping a few mints in your mouth before the interview can eliminate one problem that might create a poor initial impression; you'll have one less thing to worry about.

9. *If you carry a briefcase, be sure it's of high quality and small.* It is often better not to carry an attaché case into the interview. It's just one more thing to distract you and to remember to pick up upon leaving. However, if you have résumés or other papers that will be needed, select a case that looks good—for the same reasons you dress well. It's all part of your total appearance.

From a practical standpoint, however, it is helpful if the case is thin. Leather envelopes seem ideal. With larger briefcases, getting at and finding material can often be awkward (and hence embarrassing). Latches may not open easily, or the résumé may be mixed in with tickets or other papers so that you can't locate it easily. Thin envelopes, with no latches, make it easy for you to reach in and extract whatever material is needed.

10. *Don't wear sunglasses.* Good eye contact is important for establishing rapport with others. The interviewer needs to be able to see your eyes. Interviewers can also become suspicious, wondering what is hidden behind the shades.

Some Practical Do's and Don'ts

In addition to the general rules listed above, there are some gender-specific guidelines that can enhance your chances of making a favorable impression on your interviewer.

For women

- DO keep accessories (rings, necklaces, bracelets, earrings) simple. Use only enough to lend interest to your dress or suit.
- DO wear a business suit or conservative dress (unless the job is of a nature that requires "work" clothes).
- DON'T wear low-cut blouses or clothing that appears "sexy."
- DO go easy on makeup. Heavy makeup is often distracting.
- DON'T use heavy perfume. The safest course is something subtle or none at all.

For men

- DO keep to solid colored shirts—standard white or pale blue.
- DO keep ties on the conservative side.

- DO be careful about rings. Many interviewers will make negative judgments about rings other than wedding bands. The safest course of action is to remove all but the wedding band.
- DON'T take off your jacket unless all others are in shirt sleeves.
- DON'T wear perfumed after-shave lotion.

Neatness Is Essential

In the final analysis, your total impact should be one of *neatness:* Get a fresh haircut and styling. At interview time, check that your hair is combed and in place; your fingernails clean and cut; and your shoes polished. Clothing should look tidy—shirts or blouses tucked in properly, ties straight, and garments wrinkle-free. Many interviewers interpret a disheveled appearance as a sign of disorganization or carelessness.

For additional ideas about men's clothing, you may find John Mallory's book, *New Dress for Success* (New York: Warner Books, 1988) helpful. Since dress trends can change fairly quickly, be certain that the edition you refer to is current.

For assistance in planning your wardrobe for your various interviews, see Skill Builder 15.

SKILL BUILDER 15
Planning Your Interview Wardrobe

Looking good in the interviewer's eyes takes some thoughtful planning. In deciding how you will dress for your interviews, two basic principles should be kept in mind:

1. Dress in a style similar to that followed by people in the job and/ or organization to which you are applying. You can be a bit more dressy but should be clearly seen as fitting in.
2. Dress conservatively. Your clothing should not call attention to itself.

In Figure 7-1, I provide an opportunity for you to think through your outfits for several different interviews. Planning now may eliminate the need for last-minute hurrying out for a purchase that may not create the impression you desire.

As a final check, it might be helpful to compare your planned wardrobe against the list of Do's and Don'ts listed earlier in this chapter.

If you've followed the guidelines provided, you can go to your interview confident that you look right. You will make a good first impression!

Figure 7-1. Wardrobe checklist.

(A)

My Outfit for Interview With ______________ (name of organization)		
Clothing item	*Have—will wear*	*Need to get*
Suit/Dress		
Blouse/Shirt		
Shoes		
Tie/Accessories		
Hair Styling/Cut		
Briefcase (opt'l)		

(B)

My Outfit for Interview With ______________ (name of organization)		
Clothing item	*Have—will wear*	*Need to get*
Suit/Dress		
Blouse/Shirt		
Shoes		
Tie/Accessories		
Hair Styling/Cut		
Briefcase (opt'l)		

(continues)

Figure 7-1. (Continued)

(C)

My Outfit for Interview With ______________________ (name of organization)		
Clothing item	*Have—will wear*	*Need to get*
Suit/Dress		
Blouse/Shirt		
Shoes		
Tie/Accessories		
Hair Styling/Cut		
Briefcase (opt'l)		

(D)

My Outfit for Interview With ______________________ (name of organization)		
Clothing item	*Have—will wear*	*Need to get*
Suit/Dress		
Blouse/Shirt		
Shoes		
Tie/Accessories		
Hair Styling/Cut		
Briefcase (opt'l)		

(E)

My Outfit for Interview With ______________________________
(name of organization)

Clothing item	*Have—will wear*	*Need to get*
Suit/Dress		
Blouse/Shirt		
Shoes		
Tie/Accessories		
Hair Styling/Cut		
Briefcase (opt'l)		

Chapter 8
Building Psychological Confidence

If you feel unsure of yourself going into an interview, the anxiety will reduce your effectiveness and make it difficult to think on your feet and to speak in a relaxed, confident manner. Your feelings will be easily detected by most interviewers and will likely be interpreted as reflecting a lack of self-confidence.

Of course, everyone is a little nervous during interviews—that's only natural. In fact, mild anxiety can get your juices flowing and can result in greater alertness. Problems arise when you experience severe jitters before the interview and/or deep anxiety during the interview.

In this chapter, I explore ways to minimize anxiety levels so that you can present yourself in a confident, assured manner.

Beating the Pre-Interview Jitters

A relaxed manner is one of the most effective means of projecting an image of self-confidence. When you appear at ease, the interviewer will feel more comfortable (remember, many interviewers may be as anxious as you are), and hence you will make a better impression. In fact, assuming you are technically qualified through experience or know-how for the position you are seeking, *the degree to which the interviewer feels comfortable with you is probably the single most important determinant of your acceptability as a candidate.* So let's examine some ways to help keep your anxiety level at a comfortable point.

Getting Relaxed Before *Your Interviews*

There are several ways to reduce your pre-interview anxiety to a manageable level. Here are some time-honored techniques:

1. *Be prepared.* It's obvious. The better prepared you are, the more confident you will feel. It's like the feelings you experience before taking a school exam when you *know* you know the answers: You walk into the exam feeling peaceful and without distress. And, best of all, you are able to think clearly.

The entire first section of this book has focused on helping you to prepare for interviews. If you have completed the Skill Builders and made use of the Company Fact Sheets, you will be prepared and able to relate effectively to most interviewers.

2. *Get there early.* Allow yourself plenty of time to find the office. When you are in a strange city, it is often helpful to get the "lay of the land" by locating the building and establishing a travel route the evening before your interview.

3. *Organize your materials.* If you plan to bring papers with you (perhaps samples of past projects or extra résumés), have them neatly organized in a slim, professional-looking briefcase or large handbag. Also, it will be very helpful to have a small notebook. If you will not be carrying a briefcase, select a notebook that can easily slip into your pocket or handbag. Sometimes during the interview, the interviewer may mention a name or telephone number that is important to remember. Fumbling for paper on which to note such information will create tension and make you appear disorganized and ill at ease. For the same reason, shed your outer coat in the reception area rather than in the interview room.

4. *Reduce tension.* Feelings of tension can be substantially diminished by simple relaxation exercises. Here are two that can be done in the waiting room without calling attention to yourself. In fact, they can even be done walking down a corridor to the interviewer's office.

  a. Take a deep breath. Hold it in until the pressure becomes uncomfortable; then exhale through your mouth. Try to visualize, as you exhale, all your inner tensions being "whooshed" out as you let your breath out. Repeat this three times.
  b. Slowly clench your fists, tightening the muscles as hard as you can. Hold the muscle tension until it becomes a bit painful (about ten seconds), then slowly open your fist, letting the arm and hand muscles gradually relax.

If you have done all the preparations I have suggested, you are now ready for your interview.

Keeping Relaxed During *the Interview*

If you can conquer the before-interview jitters, it is likely that you will begin the interview appearing to be relatively relaxed and confident. But this behavior can quickly change if you are challenged or put down by the interviewer. For instance, he could make a comment such as one of these:

> "It seems to me that what you've said thus far doesn't qualify you for this level of job."
>
> "What makes you think you can handle a job like this?"
>
> "You didn't seem to succeed very well in that job. What caused you to fail?"

One way of coping with midinterview anxiety is to identify its presence and label it. At first the anxiety may only be sensed—you might experience a vague feeling that something isn't right. At that instant, say to yourself, "Here's that midinterview anxiety that Drake was talking about. I'll get over it." Simply recognizing the stress for what it is often reduces the tension.

Once identified, you can take additional steps to get yourself back into a more confident, comfortable mode. For example, public speakers with "stage fright" learn to focus on a friendly face and address their remarks to this receptive "audience." This technique is especially helpful during group interviews.

The best antidote, however, for midinterview anxiety is psychological confidence. This confidence can be attained by *knowing your strengths and being able to speak easily about them.* You need to know those attributes so well that they are instantly available to you.

A good way to get in touch with your strengths is to develop clear-cut answers to either of these questions:

- *What makes me effective at what I do?*
- *What is there about me that makes me good?*

Once you have these answers clearly fixed in your head, you will be able to cope with challenges or threatening situations without getting rattled. For example, in response to the "insufficient experience" comment from the interviewer, you can say:

> "Well, I know that I am not particularly strong in ______________, but I can compensate for that because of my strengths in ______________ and ______________."

The importance of understanding why you have been successful and being able to easily communicate that understanding cannot be overemphasized. All job applicants—even the most experienced—are vulnerable to tension if the interview takes a negative turn.

To ensure that you will be psychologically confident in all of your interviews, complete Skill Builder 16 at the end of this chapter. Right now might be a good time to start your confidence-building efforts.

THIS IS THE MOST IMPORTANT SKILL BUILDER IN THE BOOK.

It is absolutely essential that you be able to discuss your assets *with ease*—without hesitation or embarrassment. You want to feel comfortable bragging about yourself.

SKILL BUILDER 16
Building Psychological Confidence

A good way to begin this exercise is to review your answers to Skill Builder 6 (see Chapter 6). If you completed this Skill Builder, you will find it a helpful source of information about your strengths. In addition to that information, it would be worthwhile, for this exercise, to take a second look at yourself.

The questions you are attempting to answer here are:

What make me effective?

What is there about me that accounts for my successes?

To develop a clear awareness of your capabilities, think of skills and personal qualities as well as of *how* you accomplish things. For example:

"I have good problem-solving skills. When I examine a problem, I usually look at it from a 'big picture' point of view."

For now, strive to develop eight different explanations of your success.

"I am effective because I—

1. [*example*] have a high energy level—long hours are no problem for me.

2. ______________________________

____

3. ______________________________

____

4. ______________________________

____

5. ______________________________

____

6. ______________________________

____

7. ______________________________

____

8. ______________________________

____

9. ______________________________

____

Now, review your list. Eliminate or revise entries that don't ring true or are too general.

[*Example:*] "I am a good manager of people."

You may be, but it will sound weak unless you can give a specific example, such as:

"I can work well with a wide range of people—I think they see that I am sincerely interested in them and their work. If they need my time, they get it."

You should also eliminate entries that are not unidimensional. In other words, don't try to mix two skills or traits. Most people express their strengths most convincingly one at a time.

Once you have refined your list of desirable qualities, it is important to commit the items to memory. It is a good idea to make a copy of the list and refer to it from time to time—especially before any interview.

One way to gain skill in communicating strengths is to talk about them frequently—if not to someone else, to yourself as you are out driving or walking. You want to get to the point where these good qualities flow out easily and convincingly.

Then, the next time you are interviewed, you will *feel* the difference and find that midinterview stress is not an issue; you'll come across as relaxed and confident.

Section Three

During the Interview: Techniques and Strategies

Chapter 9

Waiting Room Strategies and Greeting Your Interviewer

The day for the interview has finally arrived. You're a little nervous. That's okay and normal. If you've done the preparation suggested in the previous section, you'll be ready for almost anything that comes up. If you've already had several interviews, perhaps you are feeling quite excited and positive, especially if you *know* that you can come across in a way that gains acceptance.

This section will examine the kinds of interview situations you are likely to encounter and some effective strategies for coping with them. But, first, there are some basics to consider before you actually meet your interviewer.

Waiting Room Strategies

It's generally a good idea to get to the reception room early. However legitimate your excuse for lateness may be, lack of punctuality sends out all kinds of negative vibes. On the other hand, if you are ten to fifteen minutes early, you'll have time for several potentially helpful actions. For instance, you can:

- Go to the restroom and check your appearance
- Shed and "park" any outer coat
- Ask the receptionist for the name of the interviewer (if you don't already know it)
- Skim through any company literature provided in the waiting room (to add new insights to your knowledge of the organization—particularly product or service information)
- Do your relaxation exercises

Now, you are ready! The receptionist says, "Mrs. Jones will see you now." So, here you go!

Meeting the Interviewer

The key to success is that the *interviewer must like you!* This usually means she finds you comfortable to be with and that you meet the basic requirements for the job. How do you accomplish these ends? You start by making a *good initial impression.* Here are some ways:

1. *Greet your interviewer with eye contact and a relaxed smile.* Look into the interviewer's eyes as you are greeted, not at the floor or elsewhere.

2. *Be ready to shake hands, but let the interviewer take the lead.* If the interviewer doesn't extend a hand, don't initiate the handshake. Please understand, it will not be a great faux pas if you extend your hand to shake—it's a common way to greet others in business. But if the interviewer doesn't take the initiative, there is a reason. Perhaps the interviewer feels uncomfortable with physical contact. Whatever the reason, it simply is safer to take your cue from her.

If you do shake hands, use a firm grip. While it may seem ridiculous for an interviewer to attach any significance to how you shake hands, nonetheless it does make an impact. Weak handshakes are often interpreted as revealing lack of self-confidence.

3. *Use the interviewer's name when greeting him or her.* Unless the interviewer invites you to use his or her first name, it is best to remain formal and respectful by using Mr. or Ms. This can be a little tricky with women interviewers. It is often difficult to know whether to use Ms. or Mrs. One easy way to solve the dilemma is to start by introducing yourself and then listening very carefully to how the interviewer presents her name. It typically will go like this:

> "Good morning, I'm John Drake."
>
> "Good morning, John, I'm Mrs. Johnson."

4. *Lock the interviewer's name in your memory and use it during the interview.* If you have been unable to obtain the interviewer's name before your interview and hear it for the first time when you introduce yourselves, you may well forget the name unless you make a conscious effort not to do so. There is so much going on at the beginning of an interview that the name is easily lost as you focus on other issues. A good way to lock the name in your memory is to use it several times early in the discussion. Dale Carnegie once wrote that "a man's name is to him the

sweetest and most important sound in any language." That thought is as true during an employment interview as it is in other aspects of life.

5. *Walk erect and with some vigor.* I have seen applicants create a negative first impression—even before they uttered a word. They entered the interview room slouching or shuffling, as though they had just gotten out of bed and were still half asleep. It will take a lot of convincing discussion to get the interviewer to change her initial impression that your limited vitality will be adequate to meet the demands of the job.

6. *Smile.* A smile is appealing to everyone, whereas a pan-faced or even slightly dour countenance evokes no positive vibes. Even if you're nervous, remember this is a happy occasion—you have an interview! While a constant smile would be overdoing it (and appear unnatural), a warm smile as you greet your interviewer is most appropriate.

7. *Take a seat.* But not before your interviewer sits down or offers you a chair. As you are about to sit down, consider adjusting the chair so that you don't have to face the interviewer directly, eyeball to eyeball. This act shows confidence and is likely to be more comfortable. It also allows you to demonstrate interest and attentiveness as, during the interview, you turn your head and shoulders to face the interviewer.

Sit comfortably, as far back in the chair as possible. Persons who sit on the front edge often appear tense. Sitting back will also help you feel more relaxed.

Having made a good initial impression, you now must manage yourself to your best advantage during the interview. This is the topic of Chapters 10 through 16.

Chapter 10

Getting Off to a Great Start

Some job applicants find it useful to consider the interview process from the interviewer's point of view and to develop a strategic understanding of the interviewer's needs and goals. If you are new at interviewing or want to look at the process from a strategic viewpoint, this chapter may help put things into perspective and increase your chances of success in interviews.

What Interviewers Are Looking For

Basically, interviewers seek the answers to two questions:

1. Can you do the job?
2. Are you our kind of person?

The first issue, "Can you do the job?" is a challenge for all applicants because the interviewer is concerned that you may not do what you say you can do. Your basic task, during the interview, is to help the interviewer see that *what* you do, and *how* you do it, will be an asset to the organization.

The interviewer is usually trying to find out what is not good about you. Does that seem shocking? Look at it this way. The interviewer would not be talking with you unless you already had met most of the company's requirements for the job. Undoubtedly, the interviewer screened your résumé or application form and concluded that you were at least in the ballpark. But, experience has also told him that people are not all that they appear to be. Work experiences and educational background can be distorted to look better than is actually the case. Moreover, it is not just a matter of what you have experienced or learned in the past. The interviewer is very much concerned with *how* you went about accomplishing your achievements. He wants to find out if the way you function would interfere with your ability to perform effectively or be compatible with how his company operates.

A second perspective on the interviewer's concern about your ability to do the job is that *most interviewers experience difficulty in relating your background to the job in question.* While it is true that interviewers in most human resources departments are usually experienced in interviewing, and may even have taken special training, the number of skillful interviewers you will encounter will be small. I am absolutely convinced of this, because I have spent a large portion of my professional life teaching interviewing techniques to human resources interviewers and executives. When I listen to their practice interviews, it is very clear to me that almost all jump to conclusions and have a hard time trying to understand what your past history suggests about how you will operate on the job in their company.

The interviewer's difficulty in translating past history into job behavior is a factor of great significance for any job applicant. The interviewer is constantly guessing what your statements mean. For example, suppose that while discussing your college background you mention that you were president of your fraternity. What does that mean to the interviewer? Does it mean that you are a natural leader? That you are decisive? That you are a politician who goes around apple-polishing everyone? That your father gave $25,000 to the fraternity last year? The interviewer is in a quandary about what this particular fact means for your potential job performance.

While the interpretation of data is a dilemma for the interviewer, it is a boon for the applicant. *You can help the interviewer learn that you can do the job* by describing the personal qualities or skills that made your past achievements possible. One way to help the interviewer make the necessary connections is to seek opportunities to feed him one-liners that are easy to understand and write down. The most obvious openings for such a one-liner occur when you are asked, "What are your major strengths?" or "How were you able to do so well at ______?" However, you can't depend upon being asked those particular questions; some interviewers never ask them. Instead, actively search out opportunities to communicate your strengths.

If you have completed the Skill Builders in the "Before the Interview" section, you already have at your command a wide range of good one-liners.

Here are examples of the kinds of statements I am talking about:

> "Yes, I was elected president of the fraternity. I seem to be able to relate well to all kinds of people."

"I've always been good with math and figures."

"I got that job done because I have a high energy level—long hours never bothered me."

"What helped me most on that job was developing a good staff—I've found that I have a knack for training."

What is being suggested here is not easy to do. Most people feel a bit uncomfortable talking about their good qualities. But if there was ever a time to brag, it is now! How else can you be sure that the interviewer will learn about your strengths? Remember what was said earlier about interviewers focusing on and looking for your "negatives." Here is your chance to offer the counterbalance.

It may also be helpful to think about the tremendous assistance you are providing the interviewer when you clearly spell out your strengths. Most interviewers will need to report the analysis of their interview findings to someone else. Often, they don't know what to say (except for generic statements such as "seems like a strong candidate to me"). In providing your one-liners, you have already translated past experiences into job behavior—something that most interviewers try to do but don't often succeed at. In almost all cases, *you will find that the one-line statements you provide describing your strengths will be passed on to others who may be making the final hire/not hire decision.*

An opportunity to practice weaving one-liners into your interview discussion is provided in Skill Builder 17 at the end of this chapter.

Are You Our Kind of Person?

The second major concern of the interviewer is: Will you fit in? What it comes down to is that you *need to sell yourself.*

It is essential for the interviewer to like you as a person. Interviewers are often willing to accept less qualified candidates (in terms of knowledge and experience) because they feel more comfortable with them or feel they will fit in with the organization better from the personal interaction standpoint.

We recently advertised for a professional for our human resources consulting firm. Out of approximately fifty candidates, both experienced and inexperienced, we selected one who was relatively inexperienced but who came across in the interview as warm, friendly, intelligent, and mature. We believed this applicant would be enjoyable to work with and would gain easy acceptance from our clients. We also knew that it would require significant effort to gear him up technologically, but the staff agreed that the time invested in training would be justified by having someone who fit comfortably with us.

I am sure that many of the candidates who were extremely well qualified from the technical standpoint were surprised not to receive an offer from us.

For most people, being relaxed and being yourself will help gain acceptance from interviewers. Efforts at role playing or consciously trying to impress by emphasizing characteristics that are not truly yours usually backfire. You just won't ring true in the interviewer's mind.

In the next chapter I present some techniques that will enable you to be yourself and, at the same time, communicate in ways that will establish good rapport with your interviewers.

SKILL BUILDER 17
Conveying Your Strengths—Using One-Liners

In this exercise, you will learn how to explain your strengths as you discuss your background.

You will be given an interviewer's comment that provides an opportunity for you to communicate a strength through a one-liner. Your task is to weave into your response a skill or personal quality that will interest the interviewer. To assist you in practicing this technique, a few words have been provided to get you started with your answer. I've kept the interview content reasonably generic so you can easily relate to the questions and answers.

Try to fill in the blank space with one of your strengths. A quick look at Skill Builder 16 (Chapter 8) may help you to have good answers at your fingertips.

Interviewer: Tell me about your high school experiences.

Applicant: (You): I did fairly well as far as grades are concerned; I was on the honor roll almost every term. School work came fairly easily to me, I guess because [*make up an answer that might explain how you got those good grades*] ______________________________

____.

In this exercise, notice how the accomplishment (honor roll) is then followed up by the *how.* You continually try to share, after discussing an achievement, the how or why of it. Mention what there is about you that made it possible.

In the previous example, you might have said:

> ". . . I'm good at math—the science courses came very easily to me" or, "Words come easily to me—I never found that writing exams or term papers was difficult."

Let's try some others.

Interviewer: I see that you left the job at the Johnson Company after only one year.

Applicant: Well, yes. It was a good company, but the job wasn't very challenging. I really didn't feel that it let me capitalize on my abilities. I ____

____

____.

Interviewer: How did it go in that last job of yours?

Applicant: It went quite well. I'm rather proud of the fact that I got promoted after being there only six months. I found that ______________

____

____

____.

Interviewer: What do you enjoy doing in your off-hours?

Applicant: In my spare time I enjoy ______________________

____.

[*Now see if you can weave in a positive quality or skill as you discuss your leisure time preference*]. ______________________________

____

____

You now should have a feel for what is being recommended. *Look for opportunities throughout the interview to provide one-liner descriptions of positive skills or traits.* In effect, you help the interviewer to find meaning in past performance.

Chapter 11

Selling Yourself

A big part of selling yourself rests on your ability to "read" your interviewers so that you can respond in ways that will make the interviewer feel comfortable. This means that you "talk their language"—you communicate and express yourself in a manner similar to the way the interviewer thinks and expresses herself. This is not as hard to do as you might think, once you understand *communication styles.*

Communication Styles

Every interviewer has a communication style. It is based upon the way the individual thinks and organizes his or her thoughts. There are four basic communication styles; each person typically favors one over the others. When you are interviewing someone whose communication style is similar to your own, the probability of hitting it off is good; you both speak the same language. When your styles are at variance, difficulties in relating are likely to occur.

Here's an example I recently observed. Notice how different communication styles created difficulty between these two people:

Financial analyst:	I have here the data for the warehouse project [*analyst has visible in his hands a document of about fifteen typewritten pages*], and I'd like to walk through the findings with you step by step.
Plant manager:	Never mind all the steps, Charlie. What's on the last page?
Financial analyst:	Mr. Smith, there are several options that we need to explore, and I'd like to show you how we arrived at them.
Plant manager:	Well, which option do you think is best?
Financial analyst:	I would rather not try to recommend any par-

ticular option. Each one has several pros and cons, and I think if you let me walk you through it step by step, we will see which one is best—depending on the return you want and other factors.

Plant manager: Dammit, Charlie! One of them has to be better than the others—which one do you recommend?

Financial analyst: I don't think we should do it that way. We should look at each one and . . .

Plant manager: Charlie, when you've got it figured out, come back and see me, will you?

Clearly, the thought processes of these two individuals are quite different. The plant manager is results-oriented. He skips over details and wants to get to the heart of the matter very quickly. The financial analyst, on the other hand, has a thinking and communication style characterized by logical, systematic, and orderly thinking. Imagine how differently this discussion might have gone had Charlie modified his style to be more like Mr. Smith's. He might have been quickly accepted if he had presented his thoughts this way:

Financial analyst: I've just finished the research you wanted, and I have a couple of options to show you. But the one that I believe is best will save us over $500,000 in the next fiscal year.

What Is Your Communication Style?

It is very helpful to have an awareness of how you like to think and communicate. Once this is clear, you will understand why some people are easy to relate to and some quite difficult to get through to.

Skill Builder 18, at the end of this chapter, consists of a questionnaire that will help you diagnose your style. Since it takes only a few minutes to complete, it might be helpful to do it now, before reading further. It is based on the work of Carl Jung, the famous Swiss psychologist. A more comprehensive instrument for determining communication styles is published by PEM (a division of Drake Beam Morin, Inc. in New York).

Using Communication Styles to Help You Make a Good Interview Impression

Each person has a favored communication style. You communicate best with, and are most readily accepted by, those whose communication style is similar to yours. In effect, you speak the "same language." The interviewers with whom you are most likely to experience difficulty are those whose style is different from yours—particularly if they favor your *least used style.*

The Four Basic Styles

1. *Activators.* These people have a "do-it-now" mentality. They are the doers in our world. They are concerned with end results and what is practical and tangible.

Activators are often attracted to jobs in production, professional athletics, or fast-paced work environments.

2. *Feelers.* Feelers rely on gut reactions. They are perceptive as to the needs of others, often sensing the right thing to say or do. They are people-oriented.

Feelers are often attracted to jobs in areas such as sales, human resources, and customer service.

3. *Analyzers.* Analyzers are logical, systematic, orderly, and structured. They are fact-oriented.

Analyzers are often attracted to jobs in accounting, engineering, and data processing.

4. *Conceptualizers.* Conceptualizers are concerned about future events, not the here and now. They think by intuitively linking ideas, rather than by processing them logically and deductively. As a result, conceptualizers are often innovative and creative. They are concept-oriented.

Conceptualizers are often attracted to jobs in strategic planning, academia, and advertising.

Diagnosing the Style of Your Interviewer

Once you are in the interviewer's office, you can start determining if his or her style is different from yours (which means, of course, that you will want to modify how you present yourself to be more in tune with the way your interviewer thinks). Here are four ways to diagnose the interviewer's style:

1. From the Interviewer's Desk

Activator: Cluttered and disorderly. Likely to be filled with piles of papers. Possibly two phones.

Feeler: Personal memorabilia such as family photographs and mementos from previous jobs (paper weights, pen set).

Analyzer: Neat and orderly. Sometimes almost bare, except for calculator or computer.

Conceptualizer: Piled with books. Often two piles of reports, side by side, being studied for trends.

2. *From the Interviewer's Office*

Activator: Usually appears disorganized; piles of papers everywhere. Wall hangings are strictly business (picture of the company's product); if paintings are present, they are likely to be highly action-oriented.

Feeler: Office is more informal, often personalized with pictures of family, company golf outing, diplomas, certificates, or famous quotes.

Analyzer: Surroundings rather businesslike. No frills. Charts and graphs are important giveaways. The office will be neat and tidy.

Conceptualizer: Look for bookcases filled with technical literature. Room may include intellectual toys (three-dimensional tic-tac-toe, Rubik's cube) and abstract paintings.

3. *From the Interviewer's Style of Dress*

Activator: Most incline toward simplicity. Often may not appear neat because they are so busy. Men Activators are likely to have jackets off and sleeve cuffs rolled up. Female Activators dress casually.

Feeler: Clothes are usually appropriate to work setting, but they are more on the casual side. For instance, in a business office setting, a male Feeler may wear a sport jacket unless the most acceptable dress mode is to wear a suit. Feelers are not afraid of color—bright dresses or ties are common.

Analyzer: Usually dress conservatively. Whatever is worn will look neat and tidy. Male Analyzers often will wear ties that are plain or have neat geometric designs.

Conceptualizer: Two possibilities are common: If the Conceptualizer is fashion-conscious, dress will be trendy or avant-garde. If the Conceptualizer is not concerned with fashion (more typical), dress may appear like that of stereotypical absent-minded professor—things may not quite match, for instance. For many Conceptualizers, how one dresses is a mundane issue and is relatively unimportant.

4. From the Nature of the Interviewer's Questions

Activator: Questions will focus on results accomplished—what did you do, how did you do it, how much did it contribute to profits? Questions are likely to be brief and to the point.

Feeler: Feeler is likely to spend significant amount of time in small talk. Will probably ask questions about your relationships with others—boss, subordinates, even family. Also likely to show, in the questions, an interest in you as a person, rather than simply exploring your educational or work experiences.

Analyzer: Will ask for many facts and figures—what was your grade point average? Your salary in each of your jobs? How much did your efforts contribute to profits? Questions are likely to appear businesslike and perhaps even curt.

Conceptualizer: Questions will center about your ideas and concepts—particularly about the future. Conceptualizer will not focus much on the here-and-now issues. Typical questions will begin with, "What do you think about . . . ?"

Adapting to the Style of Your Interviewer

Once it becomes apparent that your interviewer possesses a different communication style from yours, it is helpful to modify how you present yourself in order to "speak his language." Basically, you should not attempt to alter yourself in any way, except in how you organize and communicate information; tailor your answers in such a way as to be consonant with how the interviewer prefers to organize his or her thoughts.

Tailoring Your Presentation

Activator: Keep your answers short and to the point. Above all, don't ramble. Expect to be interrupted by phone calls. Try to include factual achievements and end results as you discuss your background. Emphasize your ability to get things done.

Feeler: Let the interviewer indulge in extensive small talk—participate without impatience. Emphasize your skills in working with others and the satisfactions you derive from such activities. If interviewer adopts an informal approach (e.g., uses first names), follow a similar pattern. Sharing a common family or community interest will be very appropriate.

Analyzer: Try to describe your background in a methodical, complete, and chronological manner. The Analyzer likes information presented in an organized, logical, and systematic way. Be sure to put forth facts and figures, and avoid ambiguous expressions such as "approximately" or "really did well." Avoid digressions and excessive expressions of emotion.

Conceptualizer: Avoid dwelling on the past. Talk of future goals. Whenever you can, mention new or innovative ideas you developed. Expect interviewer to go off on tangents—contribute your ideas and follow along.

If you would like practice in tailoring your way of thinking and communicating to that of your interviewers, turn to the end of the chapter for Skill Builder 19. You will probably find this exercise both fun and informative.

The concept of interviewers having different communication styles provides the basis for responding to questions in ways that will gain acceptance. A key ingredient in a successful interview is enabling the person across the desk to feel comfortable with you. This is most easily achieved by putting forth your responses in ways that match the interviewer's pattern of thinking. All it takes is a quick diagnosis of the interviewer's communication style and a few adjustments in how you present your thoughts and which of your attributes you focus on.

SKILL BUILDER 18
Diagnosing Your Communication Style

Indicate the order in which you believe each ending best describes you. Use 1 for the ending that best fits you, 2 for the one that next best fits you, 3 for the next, and 4 for the ending that is least like you.

1. I am likely to impress others as

   a. practical and to the point. a. ______
   b. emotional and somewhat stimulating. b. ______
   c. astute and logical. c. ______
   d. intellectually oriented and somewhat complex. d. ______

2. When I work on a project, I

   a. want it to be stimulating and involve lively interaction with others. a. ______
   b. concentrate to make sure it's systematically or logically developed. b. ______
   c. want to be sure it has a tangible payout that will justify my spending time on it. c. ______
   d. am most concerned about whether it breaks new ground or advances knowledge. d. ______

3. When I think about a problem, I usually

   a. think about concepts and relationships between events. a. ______
   b. analyze what preceded it and what I plan next. b. ______
   c. remain open and responsive to my feelings about the matter. c. ______
   d. concentrate on things as they are right now. d. ______

4. When confronted by others with a different point of view, I can usually make progress by

   a. getting at least one or two specific commitments for future action. a. ______

b. trying to place myself in others' shoes. b. ______
c. keeping my composure and helping others see things reasonably and logically. c. ______
d. relying on my basic ability to conceptualize and pull things together. d. ______

5. In communicating with others, I may unintentionally

a. express boredom with talk that is too detailed. a. ______
b. convey impatience with those who express ideas that they have obviously not thought through carefully. b. ______
c. show little interest in thoughts and ideas that exhibit little or no originality. c. ______
d. tend to ignore those who talk about long-range implications and direct my attention to what needs to be done now. d. ______

Analyzing Your Communication Style Questionnaire

To obtain an approximate indication of your communication style, enter the number (1, 2, 3, or 4) that you wrote next to each ending:

	Conceptualizer	*Analyzer*	*Feeler*	*Activator*
Question 1	d. ______	c. ______	b. ______	a. ______
Question 2	d. ______	b. ______	a. ______	c. ______
Question 3	a. ______	b. ______	c. ______	d. ______
Question 4	d. ______	c. ______	b. ______	a. ______
Question 5	c. ______	b. ______	a. ______	d. ______
TOTALS	______	______	______	______

Total each column. The column that has the smallest sum indicates your favored communication style; the column with the largest total is your least used style.

If your profile is relatively flat—without a clear-cut low total or high total—it may mean that you do not follow a consistent thinking and communication pattern. You probably adapt each time to the circumstances. In an interview, this will be very helpful, provided, of course, that you adapt appropriately to the style of your interviewer.

To gain some insights on how to use communication styles to your advantage, you'll need to know a little bit more about each style. Return to the discussion under ''Using Communication Styles to Help You Make a Good Interview Impression'' earlier in this chapter.

SKILL BUILDER 19
Adapting Your Interview Comments

This exercise will help you adapt your interview comments to match the communication style of your interviewer (after you have discovered that his style is different from your own).

In each example, imagine you are faced with an interviewer who prefers the communication style given. Write out a possible response.

Activator:

A. What results or accomplishments could you mention? [*For this exercise, just two or three words are necessary; don't try to spell it all out*]:

1. ______________________________
2. ______________________________
3. ______________________________
4. ______________________________
5. ______________________________

B. What could you do to remind yourself to be brief and to the point during your interview with an Activator? ______________________________

____

____

Feeler:

A. What interpersonal skills and/or people concerns could you mention when being interviewed by someone with a Feeler style?

1. ______________________________
2. ______________________________
3. ______________________________
4. ______________________________
5. ______________________________

B. What family or community interests might you keep in the back of your mind to mention should an appropriate opportunity arise?

____

____

Analyzer:

A. What specific facts or figures from your background could you call upon during your interview with an Analyzer?

Schooling: (grade point averages, class standing)

______________ ______________

______________ ______________

______________ ______________

Work History: (percent increases in sales, volume, profits; reductions in costs; grade levels advanced; dates of promotions)

Job: ______________________________

Achievement: ______________________________

Job: ______________________________

Achievement: ______________________________

Job: ______________________________

Achievement: ______________________________

Job: ______________________________

Achievement: ______________________________

Job: ______________________________

Achievement: ______________________________

B. What can you do that will keep you from going off on tangents or expressing emotions too freely? ______

______

______

Conceptualizer:

A. What have you done that is original, innovative, or unique that you can include in presenting your background to a Conceptualizer?

1. ______

______

______

2. ______

______

______

3. ______

______

______

4. ______

______

______

5. ______

______

______

How can you show the Conceptualizer your interest in the future? Consider long-term goals and concern about where the industry is going. How could you relate your skills to where the company is going?

Goals: ______

______

Concerns for the future: ______

______

Abilities that could be tied to a company's plans or goals for the future:

1. ______________________________
2. ______________________________
3. ______________________________

Chapter 12

Gatekeeping Interviews: How to Manage Them

In your employment search, you are likely to encounter five different kinds of interviews, depending upon where the interview takes place and/or the stage you are at in an organization's hiring process. Three of these can be termed *gatekeeper interviews*—each is a gateway to further interviews in the hiring process. They are:

1. The human resources department
2. The employment agency
3. The executive search firm

The two other basic types of interviews are the *semifinal*, occurring between the gatekeeping and final interview and, of course, the *final* interview—the one in which the hire/not hire decision is made.

Since you need to get past the gatekeepers before you can encounter anyone else, we'll start with them. Chapter 13 discusses ways to handle the semifinal and final interviews. For each interview situation, we will discuss what is being looked for as well as the best strategies for succeeding.

While the gatekeepers don't usually make the final decision about whether you will be hired, they typically determine whether you are in or out of the running. If you are not successful in a gatekeeper interview, you probably won't be seeing anyone else—at least not in the organization for which the gatekeeper works. In the section below, I'll discuss how to conduct yourself during the three different gatekeeper interviews.

The Human Resources Interview

As the name implies, this is the interview that takes place in the personnel department. You will not encounter it in every job-hunting situation, but it will almost always occur if you are applying for employment in a large organization.

Whom Will You Encounter?

This interview will usually be conducted by an experienced interviewer. More often than not, the interviewer will be a woman. She will usually make an effort to put you at ease but at the same time will not hesitate to bore in or ask tough questions about your background.

What Is the Interviewer Looking For?

The most helpful thing to understand about this interview is that it is fundamentally a screening interview. The interviewer will be trying to determine if your background is all that your résumé or application form says it is. Your primary job will be to get past this screen to the people who will actually make the hiring decision. Typically, the human resources interviewer has the power to reject you but not to hire you.

In most cases, the human resources interviewer is not likely to have a sophisticated understanding of the technology required in the position for which you are being interviewed. Rather, she is working from a job description or list of important requirements provided by the hiring manager. She wants to be sure that you meet *basic* requirements. The interviewer will also be alert to any behavior on your part that will not sit well with people in the department in which the job is located.

It is helpful to understand the problems confronted by this interviewer. First of all, she usually has a large number of people to interview in a day, so she is often pressured by time. Second, she doesn't want to embarrass herself. This could easily happen if, after screening, she refers a candidate forward who obviously does not meet the job specifications. So, in effect, the interviewer hopes that:

- You will pass the screen so that, at last, the job will be filled and further interviewing for it will no longer be necessary.
- You meet at least the minimum experience and knowledge requirements.
- You are reasonably presentable (no obvious turnoffs).

How to Make the Best Impression During the Human Resources Interview

When you consider the time issue and the screening nature of the human resources interview, the approach you adopt as applicant is fairly clear.

1. *Be prepared to present key factual data about your background.* As you review your work history, be sure of your dates of employment, earnings, and at least one significant accomplishment in each job.

2. *Err by being too brief rather than too complete.* This interviewer usually doesn't have a lot of time to spend with you. Moreover, the more you say, the more likely you are to reveal some disqualifying red flag. Respond directly to the questions asked, but don't volunteer additional data.

3. *Let the interviewer control the pace and discussion climate.* Don't try to take charge or make a strong impression from the personality standpoint. It's too risky in this interview. If you're bland but nothing is dramatically wrong, the interviewer will pass you on to the next stage in the employment process. But if something rubs her the wrong way, this may be your last interview at this particular company.

4. *Be concise and to the point.* This applies even if you are asked open-ended questions such as those listed in Chapter 6. (Although your interviewer is likely to focus on essential facts, she may well throw in one or two of the "twelve tough questions" we discussed in that part of the book.)

The Employment Agency Interview

It is helpful to understand that employment agencies, or contingency search firms, operate on a commission basis. If they refer you to an organization and the company hires you, they get paid—anywhere from 10 percent to 30 percent of your starting salary. For most of them, it's a contingency arrangement; they get their fee only if you are hired and work out well. The more people they see and refer to prospective employers, the more money they can make. For this reason, these interviews, for the most part, are going to be brief (thirty minutes or less).

There are three different kinds of agencies you may encounter:

1. *Industry agencies.* As the name implies, these agencies specialize in jobs in specific types of organizations such as banks, law firms, chemical companies, or retail outlets.
2. *Functional agencies.* These focus on jobs of a particular nature such as data processing, personnel, or sales.
3. *General agencies.* These agencies attempt to find viable candidates for a wide range of industries and/or jobs.

These three different kinds of agencies are mentioned because the interviews may differ, depending on whether the agency is specialized or not. Your interviews at the generalized agencies are likely to be less demanding but explore broader aspects of your background.

Whom Will You Encounter?

Interviewers in most agencies are experienced; they have interviewed a large number of job applicants. In most agencies—general or specialized—interviewing is a pressure-packed job and the turnover is high. Typically, the interviewers are young and aggressive. Occasionally, especially in agencies that specialize, you may encounter an experienced old-timer who knows his clients or industry very well and who knows exactly what he wants to learn about you.

What Is the Interviewer Looking For?

In nonspecialized employment agencies, interviewers are looking for almost any skills or experiences that are marketable. Unlike a human resources interviewer, the agency interviewer hopes you can qualify for job openings he knows about (or hopes to learn about). He is trying to fit you into a job rather than screen you out.

The interview is likely to be characterized by an initial perusal of your résumé or the agency's own background form. A few brief, pertinent questions are likely to be asked in order to flesh out particular aspects of your training or experience. If the interviewer notices something of interest, you can expect a number of follow-up questions on that specific area of your background.

These second-tier questions are usually derived from the client's description of desired capabilities. Thus, in most agency interviews, you will find the interviewer fairly abrupt, focused, and very much in control. For the most part, he will be seeking factual data. Once he believes that you meet the minimum qualifications, he may then direct his attention toward your personal qualities and the kind of impact you will have on the agency's client.

Interviews in specialized agencies (industry or functional) will be similar in character to those described for the generalized agencies, with two exceptions: (1) They could be quite *brief*—if you are not technically qualified for the specialty they serve, you will be given a polite but quick "goodbye"; and (2) if they see you as qualified, the probing about your background—particularly your technical skills—is likely to be extensive.

How to Make a Good Impression During Your Employment Agency Interviews

1. *Be prepared to discuss your technical qualifications succinctly.* Since these interviews will center around your technical qualifications, it is essential that you be able to mention readily the kinds of things you can do. For each job you have had, you need to be able to explain what you

know how to do; for example, on your current job you may use a personal computer and know how to use Excel spreadsheet software.

2. *Don't be surprised if the interview is intimidating.* As I've mentioned, most of these interviewers are aggressive and under significant time pressure. Their abruptness can easily be disconcerting. Being aware that this quick, probing kind of interview may confront you enables you to adopt a tougher posture going into the interview. Remember, in these interviews, agency personnel are hoping you are good enough so that they can forward your résumé to their client. They want you as much as you need them.

3. *Be ready to take charge.* If it appears that the interview is slipping away from you, it will be necessary to take decisive action if you hear the interviewer make a statement like this:

> "I'm sorry, but we don't have anything right now that matches your qualifications. But you've got a good track record, and we'll keep your résumé in our active files."

At this point, you have to step in and intervene. In the interviewer's rapid perusal of your résumé, he may have overlooked specific skills or experiences. It's now up to you to make certain they are known. Here's an example of the kind of intervention I am suggesting:

> "Before we end this interview, I was wondering if you realize that in my last job at Citizen's Bank I made over one hundred commercial loans. I approved home mortgages and supervised eight tellers and two assistant managers. I really know the banking business and how to go out and get new customers. In fact, in the two years I was there, I increased deposits by over a half million."

If you can help the interviewer become aware of some marketable skills he overlooked, he'll thank you for it; he now might be able to make a referral and a sale. So there is nothing to lose; show the agency interviewer why prospective employers might find you worthwhile to meet.

The Executive Recruiter Interview

Working with executive recruiters is a complicated matter. There are so many possible points of contact and possible agendas that one could easily write a book on this topic alone. In this section, therefore, I discuss only the executive recruiter interviews you are most likely to experience.

Executive recruiters work on a very different basis from most agencies. They are hired by their clients to find candidates, and they are paid whether they fulfill the search or not. The most reputable search firms do not work on a contingency basis. Thus, the extent of their interest in you, and their consequent interview approach, is quite different from what you will encounter in an employment agency or contingency firm. If you get an interview at an executive search firm, you will definitely have to sell yourself. In the sections below, I discuss how best to manage two different interview situations—the first, if you have initiated the interview; the second, if the recruiter has called you.

Whom Will You Encounter?

Among the firms belonging to the Association of Executive Search Consultants and at other large search firms, the interviewers you meet are likely to be experienced, competent, and polished. A high proportion will be men; very often they will have been successful executives who formerly worked in the corporate world.

What Is the Interviewer Looking For?

The answer to this question depends upon how you got to the interview in the first place.

1. *You have contacted the recruiter.* If you have initiated the contact and have been granted an interview, either you struck a responsive chord with the recruiter (via résumé or phone conversation) and he sees a possibility of your meeting a client need or he is giving you a courtesy interview—perhaps because your firm retains this recruiter, you've known the recruiter from the past, or you've been referred to him by an influential friend.

If your presence in the interview represents a courtesy gesture, the interviewer is not likely to be looking for anything but a tactful way to ease you out. Help in preparing for this interview can be found in Skill Builder 21.

If your interview is in response to information you have previously provided, the interviewer will be attempting to see if you are qualified and presentable. We'll discuss the ins and outs of managing this interview in the next section.

2. *The recruiter has initiated the contact with you.* If the recruiter calls you, you should learn, *before* the interview, what the recruiter is looking for. This is important because his objectives can vary greatly, from wanting to know you as a contact (so that you might employ him or his firm for a future search) to wanting to see how closely you qualify for a retainer search assignment.

The way you determine the real purpose of your recruiter's interview is to qualify his objectives during the initial phone conversation. For an excellent presentation of strategies to use during this phone call, see John Lucht's book *Rites of Passage at $100,000+* (New York: The Viceroy Press, 1988).

The Self-Initiated Interview

How you present yourself in your initial executive search interview is determined by the reason you were granted the interview. If the recruiter has a definite position in mind and wants to know more about you, see the next section, "The Recruiter-Initiated Interview."

On the other hand, if the recruiter granted you a "let's get-acquainted," courtesy interview, you must take a different approach because it is unlikely that you will match a position the recruiter is presently trying to fill. In this situation, your goal is to present yourself as an attractive candidate worth remembering for a *future* search. Here's how to do it.

How to Make a Good Impression During Your Interview With an Executive Recruiter

1. *Remember, the interview is likely to be short.* No more than thirty minutes. After all, you're not a candidate. This means you have to avoid detail, be sensitive to the interviewer's cues about when a subject area is finished, and take the initiative in ending the meeting—maybe even before the thirty minutes are up.

2. *You have to make a good initial impression.* The interviewer is not likely to delve very deeply into your background, so it's necessary to create an aura of success. You do this by getting across three points:

a. *You have valuable experience.* You've accomplished things that mark you as a success or an innovator. For instance:

"During my stint at General Foods, I conceived the whole new line of after-dinner coffees and brought them to market. In the first year, those sales added more than $2 million to the bottom line.

b. *You have a good track record.* You've progressed at an above-average rate and/or have an impressive list of achievements.
c. *You have the characteristics of a successful executive.* You generally communicate this idea by your behavior during the interview. However, your image can be enhanced by an occasional reference to an effective executive trait or personal quality.

The ability to communicate effectively—being pleasant, yet to the point—is probably the single most significant behavioral skill to display.

Effective personal qualities can be subtly communicated by tying them to an achievement. For example:

> "Well, that job involved a tremendous amount of travel—especially international—but I have a high energy level and I was able to cope with it quite well."

If you will be visiting a retainer search firm, Skill Builder 21 will help you get organized to make a good impression.

The Recruiter-Initiated Interview

Much of what has been said throughout this book about presenting yourself effectively in employment interviews also applies to recruiter-initiated interviews. But, in addition, you must come across as one who "looks the part." This means that you communicate well, dress the part, and are socially adroit. If you lack these surface attributes, the recruiter is not likely to spend much time delving into your accomplishments.

How do you create such a favorable impression? First of all, you can recognize that you are the buyer. The recruiter is pursuing you. If you appear either too eager or too passive, the effect will not be good. Probably the best procedure is to find out if what the recruiter has is of real interest to you (assuming, for the moment, that you didn't ascertain this in prior telephone conversations).

Whether or not you will be interested usually depends on two factors:

1. Does he really have a position for which he is conducting a bona fide search?
2. Is the position a good career opportunity for you?

The recommended strategy then is to come across as a strong candidate by tactfully taking charge and asking questions, while simultaneously selling yourself. "Selling yourself" has been discussed throughout this book, so I focus here on the taking charge/asking questions aspect of your interview.

One way to place yourself in the role of a buyer is to approach the interview with the purpose of determining whether or not what the recruiter has is worth your time. The easiest way to do this is by asking questions, even at the outset of the interview. (Of course, I am overstating the point here a bit. Obviously, if you've qualified the search firm's interest in you via previous telephone discussions, you are at the interview because you believe there is something to be gained. So it is still necessary to sell yourself despite your buyer mentality.)

Here are a few examples of questions that help you take charge. Start with getting a sense of expectations:

> "Just so I can pace myself, how much time do we have?"
>
> "Do you want me to start by talking about myself, or can we start by talking about the position? I have a few questions I'd like to ask you."

Be prepared with clear-cut questions about what you need to know. For example:

> "What is the exact job title?"
>
> "To whom will I report?"
>
> "Could you tell me about the location?"
>
> "How many subordinates?"
>
> "What can you tell me about the compensation?"

If you have completed Skill Builder 4, you already have a good core of questions to ask your executive recruiter.

If the position is not sufficiently attractive, be straightforward about your reactions. It reveals strength on your part, and you might even set yourself up as an attractive candidate for a better assignment in the future. Here's an example of such a comment:

> "As I'm listening to your comments about the position, it seems to me that my current assignment offers me even more potential. Right now I report directly to the vice-president of marketing. He's already stated that he's going to take early retirement, and I'm the most logical candidate. My three product lines have shown the fastest growth of all those under his wing, so he's been grooming me for the job."

If it appears that the recruiter is favorably impressed with you and you are interested in the job, your objective is to keep the exploration going, perhaps by attempting to set up another meeting. If you have determined that you're a finalist and you want to explore the opportunity further, then this is the time to press for the company name, explaining that you want to begin preparing for your meeting with the client.

SKILL BUILDER 20
Interviewing With Employment Agencies

In employment agency interviews, it is important to be able to mention quickly what you can do. It is not simply a matter of discussing job responsibilities, although these are important. In agency interviews, mentioning *specific abilities* helps the interviewer to see more clearly how your talents can be presented to his client.

In the following spaces, for each job or educational experience that you have had, try to describe, in a one-liner, what the experience or training enables you to do.

WORK EXPERIENCES:

Job With ______________________________

What I can do: 1. ______________________________

2. ______________________________

3. ______________________________

4. ______________________________

Job With ______________________________

What I can do: 1. ______________________________

2. ______________________________

3. ______________________________

4. ______________________________

Job With ______________________________

What I can do: 1. ______________________________

2. ______________________________

3. ______________________________

4. ______________________________

Job With ______________________________

What I can do: 1. ______________________________

2. ______________________________

3. ______________________________

4. ______________________________

EDUCATIONAL EXPERIENCES

School: ______________________________

Learned that I can: 1. ______________________________

2. ______________________________

3. ______________________________

School: ______________________________

Learned that I can: 1. ______________________________

2. ______________________________

3. ______________________________

School: ______________________________

Learned that I can: 1. ______________________________

2. ______________________________

3. ______________________________

School: ______________________________

Learned that I can: 1. ______________________________

2. ______________________________

3. ______________________________

Do a quick check on what you've written. Do your one-liners clearly describe tangible skills? Revise or eliminate any that could not readily be applied in some job situation. For example, "I'm good at business math" could be improved by explaining *what* you can do mathematically, for example, "I know how to develop a balance sheet and profit and loss statement."

Before any agency interview, review this Skill Builder so that you can easily discuss your specific job capabilities. They may open a number of new possibilities for you.

SKILL BUILDER 21
Preparing for a Courtesy Interview

Your goal in this brief interview is to make an impression that leads the recruiter to call you in the future. During the interview you will try to leave an impression of competence. Here are three areas that can help convey that you are the kind of executive the recruiter will want to keep on tap:

1. *Valuable experience:* What specifically have you accomplished that marks you as a success or innovator? (Mention no more than three items.)

Accomplishment 1: ______________________________

What was the end result? ______________________________

____

Why was it important? ______________________________

____

Accomplishment 2: ______________________________

What was the end result? ______________________________

____

Why was it important? ____________________

____

Accomplishment 3: ____________________

What was the end result? ____________________

____

Why was it important? ____________________

____

2. *A good track record.* Can you point to a series of advances or promotions that reflect another executive's confidence in you? The spaces below may help organize your thinking on this issue.

a. *Was there a company in which you advanced one or more levels?* Yes _____ No _____ (If No, move on to B.)

If Yes, Name of Company: ____________________
Was the advancement at an above-average rate?
Yes _____ No _____
If Yes, list the job titles in order of progression:

Job A ____________________

Job B ____________________

Job C ____________________

What was it that your superiors saw in you that led them to move you ahead so rapidly? "What they saw in me was ____________________

____

____________________."

The answer to "what they saw in me" should be a succinct one-liner, for instance, "my ability to step in and take responsibility. The job wasn't getting done, so I did it."

If you checked No to the "above average-rate" question, your advancement is probably not worth mentioning to the recruiter.

b. *Were there instances when you moved from one organization to another and made a significant upward leap—either in job level or degree of responsibility?* Yes _____ No _____

If Yes, Name of Organization ______________________________

What made the move significant? ______________________________

____

The job level increased from ______________________________
(job title)

to ______________________________

The scope of responsibility increased from ______________________________

____
(number of persons managed, size of budget, size of company, etc.)

to ______________________________

____

What made you attractive to the new employers?

"I was attractive to them because they saw me as being able to

____

______________________________."

In case there were two such moves, additional space is provided below:

What was the move? Name of Organization ______________________________

What made the move significant? ______________________________

____

The job level increased from ______________________________
(job title)

to ______________________________

The scope of responsibility increased from ______________________________

____
(number of persons managed, size of budget, size of company, etc.)

to ______________________________

____

What made you attractive to the new employers?

"I was attractive to them because they saw me as being able to

____

______________________________."

3. *Personal characteristics.* In this section you will prepare yourself so as to help the recruiter see you as solid executive material. Of course, your general demeanor during the interview will speak the loudest on this subject. But you can add to this impact by mentioning two or three admirable executive qualities. These descriptions come across best when they are woven into your comments about your work experiences or achievements.

Here is an example that was cited in the text:

> "Well, that job involved a tremendous amount of travel—especially international—but I have a high energy level and I was able to do it."

Personal Quality 1:

Name an achievement ______________________

What personal executive quality made it possible? (decisiveness? big-picture outlook? drive?) ______________________

____

Personal Quality 2:

Name an achievement ______________________

What personal executive quality made it possible? (decisiveness? big-picture outlook? drive?) ______________________

____

Personal Quality 3:

Name an achievement ______________________

What personal executive quality made it possible? (decisiveness? big-picture outlook? drive?) ______________________

____

This exercise should help you get all the significant "track record" information organized so that you can comfortably discuss this aspect of your background. It will be helpful to review this Skill Builder shortly before your recruiter interviews.

Chapter 13

The Semifinal and Final Interviews: How to Manage Them

Once you have gained the approval of a gatekeeping interviewer, one of two things may happen: (1) You will be referred to someone who will interview you in order to make the final hire/not hire decision, or (2) you will be conducted through a series of interviews with a variety of interviewers. Since these two kinds of interview situations involve rather different dynamics, I discuss them separately.

Let's start with the series of interviews because often it serves as another level of gatekeeping before you get to the final decision maker. I refer to this interview process as the beauty parade.

Beauty Parade Interviews

Each of these interviews is likely to be scheduled for a half hour to an hour's duration. In a typical day you might be involved in as many as seven such interviews; a luncheon session may be included as well.

I have cataloged the beauty parade as a semifinal interview because, typically, you must get a consensus approval from these interviewers before you meet the individual who makes the final decision. Sometimes the decision maker is among the beauty parade interviewers; you may or may not be told beforehand who that individual is. In any case, after these interviewers have seen you, they must compare their assessments of you and decide whether to make you an offer or to pass you on to the decision maker.

Whom Will You Encounter?

The interviewers participating in the beauty parade may include people who'll be your superiors or peers in the department where you'll be employed, as well as key managers in work areas with which your department will interact. It is very common, for example, for someone who is being hired as head of data processing to meet with the vice-presidents and/or department heads of the various groups that the data processing department serves.

Most of these individuals find interviewing a difficult chore; largely untrained, they are uncomfortable in the role of interviewer. They also may resent the intrusion of the interview into the midst of their busy workday—especially if you will not be a member of their department. Moreover, as is the situation with human resources interviewers, they have the burden of providing someone else (usually their boss or the human resources department) with their analysis of your suitability.

What Beauty Parade Interviewers Are Looking For

It's not easy to pinpoint what interviewers are after. You may be confronted with as many different approaches as there are interviewers. Having said that, some trends do exist. As a rule, beauty parade interviewers are interested in two things:

1. *Level of competence.* Can you do the job? Members of the department where you'll be assigned will focus heavily on your work experience. They will have many questions about what you did and how you went about achieving your past accomplishments. Remember, since most of these individuals are untrained interviewers, they will feel most comfortable focusing on shop talk.
2. *Fit.* A second question on the minds of the interviewers will be, "Can I get along with this person? Is this the kind of person I can live with?" This concern, often unspoken, frequently overrides all others. You'll be the new kid on the block, and each and every interviewer in the beauty parade will be trying to determine your specific impact on him or her.

How to Make the Best Impact During the Beauty Parade

A good overall guideline for making a favorable impression during the interview series is to make sure you don't say anything that will threaten or alienate your interviewers. Be careful about discussing changes you will make once you've come on board. Instead, stress an interest in being of help to each interviewer and his department. When it seems appropriate, you could mention an example of how your willingness to pitch in and help worked out well in your last job.

As far as compatibility is concerned, try to maintain a comfortable rapport by being alert to your interviewers' communication styles (see

Chapter 11). During the beauty parade interviews, more than in others, judgments will be based on the comfortableness of your fit. This is where your warmth and spontaneity need to be evident. It may not be too difficult to convey a sense of compatibility once you've been through two or three of the interviews; you'll get to know the company and will most likely feel at home in the situation. Using your relaxation techniques immediately before the first few interviews could be helpful in putting you at ease.

Another guideline is to be alert and take your cues from the interviewer. If she wants to talk about your last job, talk about your last job. But this doesn't mean that you can't work in other significant points directly related to the topic at hand.

Suppose, for example, you've gleaned from earlier beauty parade interviewers that the last incumbent in the job provided little or no training for subordinates and that this created a significant number of problems. Even though your current interviewer is asking questions about the customers you dealt with in your last job, you may want to look for opportunities to mention your achievements in developing and training staff. You might, for instance, illustrate how one of your subordinates made a sale because he used a new strategy learned in one of your training sessions.

It is worth remembering, during the beauty parade, to interject, whenever feasible, the one-liners about your attributes. Like the human resources interviewers, most of these interviewers will need to develop a written assessment, or at least a verbal report, based on their evaluation of you. This commentary will be difficult for them, especially if they have spent most of the interview discussing your work experiences. So, *help them with their assessment* (Chapter 10 has already shown you how to develop these one-liners).

Here are two examples:

> "I've always been good at developing staff—I like the training aspect of managing."
>
> "I've got a high energy level—long hours really don't trouble me."

In summary, during the beauty parade interviews you will need to convey two impressions:

1. You're a good person—likable and enjoyable to work with.
2. You know your stuff. You could be helpful. If you don't pass muster in either of these two areas, you'll never get to the final, decision-making interview.

The Final Interview

This is the interview with the person in the corner office—the individual who will make the hire/not-hire decision. In most cases, if you are hired, this person will be your immediate superior or your boss's boss.

The focus of this interview is usually quite different from the others I've discussed. You've already been screened and approved. The human resources representative has passed you on, and enough of the beauty parade interviewers have judged you favorably that you arrive at this interview with one foot already in the door. Now the focus is not so much on screening out as on how you will fit in.

What the Final Interviewer Is Looking For

Let's begin this section with a comment about what the interviewer is *not* looking for. He is not looking for an in-depth discussion about your technical skills. Unless the job for which you are applying involves high technology or research, he will assume that other staff members have already explored your technical background in sufficient depth. He *is* looking for three things:

1. The central question on the mind of the final interviewer is, how will you fit in? How will you mesh with the team? If his judgment is positive, then his evaluation of your potential for advancement may become the next key issue.
2. Another area of focus for final interviewers concerns any problems that surfaced during earlier interviews (human resources or beauty parade). Earlier evaluations will have been forwarded to this interviewer, and he will want to check out some points for himself—particularly any areas that have raised question marks or doubts in the minds of previous interviewers.
3. Finally, there is the "chemistry" issue. Do you think and act in ways that are compatible with this manager's personality?

One CEO I know rejected candidate after candidate who had already been carefully screened by us (as consultants) and by his own staff. These applicants had the required work and educational backgrounds, as well as the personal qualities that were deemed desirable for the job.

When I asked the CEO why the applicants were not satisfactory, his initial response was that "their view of business was not in line with mine." This puzzled me until, after further discussion, it emerged that the applicants' responses about their executive role and where the industry was going were not sufficiently global.

It turned out that this CEO was very much a conceptual thinker. In terms of our communication styles, he was a classic Conceptualizer. In fact, he was a Conceptualizer's Conceptualizer! He looked at problems and issues from a broad, long-range, futuristic viewpoint. Any applicant who focused on the here-and-now or failed to discuss topics from a broad, conceptual standpoint was judged as being too narrow in his thinking and was rejected.

How to Make the Best Impact During the Final Interview

Try to avoid the trap of volunteering extensive information about what you've done or how you've done it. Of course, when questions about knowledge or experience arise, you will respond to them. But when this happens, answer each question as concisely as possible. In most instances, focus on significant accomplishments, rather than on details about how they were achieved. Remember, the final interviewer's primary concern is not likely to be your technical competence.

It is with your final interviewer that your preparation—especially the data you gathered on your Company Fact Sheet—will pay off the most. This interviewer is likely to be quite interested in your knowledge of the company and your awareness of current trends in its industry. Think of how favorably you will come across if you *speak about the business as though you were already employed* by the company. Try to describe how its concerns and enthusiasms are your concerns and enthusiasms.

With this interviewer it is also essential that you speak positively about the organization and people you've met (assuming you want the job). You can usually work in these kinds of comments because you are likely to be asked such questions as:

> "What are some of your reactions to what you've seen thus far?"
> "How did our team strike you?"
> "You'll be working for Mary Smith. How did that interview go?"

It is vital that you make direct, overt statements about how impressed you were with the team you met. Don't forget that these are "his people"; it is quite likely that he selected them. Try to be specific. It's better to say:

> "I was really impressed with how openly they spoke about their department problems and how Mike, Nancy, and William pitch in and help each other."

Than it is to say:

> "I was really impressed with the teamwork that takes place here."

Sometimes, as you proceed through the beauty parade, an interviewer may impress you as out of place or incompetent compared with the other employees you've met. If the final interviewer asks about your reactions to the people you've met, you are then faced with a ticklish dilemma. On the one hand, it is advantageous to be positive about what you've observed; on the other hand, there is the issue of your credibility. You don't want to be judged as naïve or a Pollyanna. It's quite possible, too, that the interviewer is attempting to evaluate your openness or your judgment about the capability of others.

There is more to be gained by being honest about your observations than by playing it cool. If asked a direct question, you can minimize your risk by making your response sufficiently vague so that it elicits additional comments from your interviewer. In this way, you can gain helpful insights about how much more it's appropriate to mention. For example:

Interviewer: What do you think of the people you've met thus far?

Applicant: I was very much impressed by all of the staff—everyone seemed highly committed and excited about the future of the firm. The only one who seemed to view things a little differently was Bill Smith.

It was mentioned earlier that your final interviewer may have had feedback from prior interviewers, perhaps even some negative reactions. There is not much you can do to prepare for this segment of your discussion because it is so difficult to guess what kinds of issues may have been raised. However, if you have time between your beauty parade interviews and the final one, it is worthwhile to review the earlier interviews to see if you can recall any discussion topics or any of your statements that appeared to make the interviewer uncomfortable. You can then try to think about effective ways of defusing any negative implications.

Also, there is no way you can be aware of all of the biases or hidden agendas that interviewers bring into interview situations. But by not monopolizing the discussion, by listening carefully to the nature of the questions, and by using the communication style techniques discussed in Chapter 11, you can become more aware of the interviewer's expectations and enhance the probability of positive chemistry.

Chapter 14

Nontraditional Interviews: How to Manage Them

Imagine arriving for what you expect will be a one-on-one interview only to find yourself in a conference room surrounded by five or six people, all intent on "dissecting" you.

This approach to assessment is only one of a variety of nontraditional interviews you may encounter. Fortunately, if you have practiced the skills we've talked about in this book, you are likely to come through with flying colors.

Most of the attributes you need to demonstrate for these unusual interviews are the same as those for traditional interviews—good appearance, a confident knowledge of your strengths, poise, and controlled enthusiasm. However, as we'll see, nontraditional interviews will require you to display some additional qualities. We'll take a look at the following three interview situations and show you how to succeed:

1. Panel interviews
2. Behavioral interviews
3. Situational interviews

Panel Interviews

What They're Like

During a panel interview you're questioned by three to six persons at the same time, so that it may often be an intimidating experience.

In most situations, the panelists will not be sophisticated interviewers. Typically, the panels are comprised of your prospective boss, perhaps your boss's boss, a human resources representative, a potential co-worker, and a manager or two from closely aligned departments. For technical jobs, subject matter experts are often included.

The interview format is typically as follows:

1. Panel members introduce themselves.
2. A few "ice-breaking" comments are made.
3. You are asked a few broad, background questions such as:

"Will you give us a brief description of your educational and work experiences?"

"What are your responsibilities in your current [or last] job?"

"What is there about this position that appeals to you?"

4. The remainder of the interview is likely to include one or both of the following questioning patterns:

a. Each panelist asks his favorite questions so that the questioning is rarely in a logical order and covers a wide variety of topics. Frequently, these questions require you to explain how you would respond to hypothetical situations. For example, you might be asked, "Suppose you had two subordinates who did not get along with each other. What, if anything, would you do about it?"
b. You are asked carefully planned, structured questions designed to evaluate your technical skills or personal qualities such as leadership potential, planning ability, or conceptual skills.

5. You will then be asked if you have any questions.

6. You will be provided with data about the job and the company. (Sometimes this information is given to you before you are asked if you have questions).

7. After about an hour, the conclusion will be signaled by a panelist—usually the human resources representative—saying something like, "Thank you so much for being with us today." Be alert for this cue because, at times, the ending may seem abrupt.

8. After your departure, the panelists will discuss your qualifications and make their ratings. In most cases, you will not receive immediate feedback as to the impression you have made.

The questioning procedure varies greatly from panel to panel. Sometimes the discussion is orderly, with each panelist taking a turn at asking questions; at other times it will appear disorganized, with panelists asking you questions almost on impulse and often interrupting one another. Occasionally, both patterns are used by the same panel—often intentionally so as to observe how you handle changes in proceedings.

In some settings you will find that the panelists are trained in behavioral interviewing, competency interviewing, or the hypothesis method. These panelists will conduct an orderly interview having a definite pattern. We'll talk more about this type of interview in the section headed "Behavioral Interviews."

In almost all panel interviews, you can expect abrupt shifts in topics. Quite often you will not be given adequate time to fully express your thoughts about a particular topic.

Where You Will Encounter Panel Interviews

Panel interviews are common in academia, government agencies (where they are called board interviews), and occasionally in corporate settings.

Organizations sometimes use panels when you are a candidate for several departments. In this way, all potential hirers can screen you, and those who are most interested can conduct additional, follow-up interviews.

Other organizations using this approach believe that having a variety of interviewers with different backgrounds helps to ensure that nothing important is left unexplored.

How to Succeed With Panel Interviews

Let's face it, panel interviews are performances. You don't have the option of "reading" your interviewer and having ten to fifteen minutes in which to establish rapport. In most cases, the focus will be on breadth rather than depth.

If you are articulate and at ease in front of a group, your panel interview might even turn out to be an enjoyable encounter. It can be a heady experience to observe that the panel is "with you"—that you're in control and the atmosphere is friendly and relaxed.

If, on the other hand, coping with abrupt questions, speaking in front of a group, and thinking quickly without preparation are not your strengths, then some practice would be most helpful.

One way to practice is to ask family or friends to act as a mock panel. Instruct them to interrupt and ask a variety of questions. Practice trying to make smooth transitions between disconnected topics. You can also work on maintaining eye contact with each interviewer and the group.

Suggestions for Managing the "Perfect" Panel Interview

1. *Network.* If you know that you will be facing a panel interview, see if through networking you can learn the focus of the questions or this corporation's typical agenda.

2. *Learn as much about the company—its goals and management style—as possible.* Such information will help you to avoid saying the "wrong thing," but, equally important, it will allow you to highlight those attributes that will encourage the panelists to see you as "their kind of person." For example, if the organization is known for its demanding work schedules, think of the times you have demonstrated a high energy level or willingness to work long hours. Then, make a conscious effort to mention such examples during your responses to questions.

3. *When you are first introduced to panel members, ask each member for his or her business card.* Array them in front of you to mirror where each one is seated. If obtaining the cards is awkward, use a notepad to draw a simple seating diagram with each panelist's name in place. Mentioning each interviewer's name contributes to creating a positive impression.

4. *Be totally familiar with your résumé.* Most of the interviewers are likely to use it as a springboard. Practice beforehand how you will explain each educational and job change.

5. *Don't be afraid to ask questions or to be "up front" about what you observe during the interview.* Speaking with confidence can help create a favorable impression. For example, if you sense that your interview is not going well, that perhaps somewhere along the way you answered inappropriately, you could say, "I sense that the atmosphere is not very positive right now. Is there something I've said, or not said, that was different from what you hoped for?" Then listen and acknowledge the feedback. You can clarify or explain whatever issue was raised, but don't argue.

6. *Maintain good eye contact with each of your questioners.* As you are responding, make brief eye contact with the other panelists too.

7. *Be positive.* As with one-on-one interviews, seek opportunities to mention your positive attributes.

Behavioral Interviews

What They're Like

These interviews are usually conducted one-on-one.

If you can visualize an interview in which you are consistently asked to describe how or why you performed certain job tasks or made particular decisions, you will have a sense of what a behavioral interview is like.

Typical questions are:

> "You said that you are 'good with people.' What is it that you do that enables you to work effectively with others?"

"What was the most difficult challenge you had to face in your last job? What did you do to overcome it?"

Behavioral interviewers want to learn how you function and what motivates you. Rarely will they provide a job description beforehand or "telegraph" the characteristics they are seeking to assess (even though they will have a job description and will have identified specific skills and qualities necessary for success).

Because most of the questions are open-ended and require you to describe actions or thoughts, behavioral interviews tend to be long, often lasting over an hour.

Interviewers using this kind of approach are likely to be trained in my "Hypothesis Method" (*The Effective Interviewer,* New York: AMACOM, 1989) or other competency-based methods. These techniques direct the interviewer to get behind the facts of your background in such a way that it's difficult for you to get away with vague or canned responses.

Where You Will Encounter Behavioral Interviews

Almost anywhere. This method of interviewing represents the current state of the art and is increasingly used in sophisticated organizations. Behavioral techniques are most likely to be encountered in final, rather than screening, interviews.

How to Succeed With Behavioral Interviews

Good news! These interviews are ideal for the techniques taught in this book. The open-ended nature of the interviewer's questions will enable you to easily mention your attributes and describe your strengths. With luck, you'll encounter many behavioral interviews.

But you can run into trouble. You can quickly find yourself in difficulty if you try to bluff. Good behavioral interviewers will always probe past generic answers to get at specifics. For example:

Interviewer: How were you able to succeed in that difficult situation?

You: I was able to get the others to cooperate and work as a team.

Interviewer: I see, but what did you do specifically that enabled you to gain their cooperation?

So, how do you get around such difficulties and avoid the potential pitfalls? There are ways:

Suggestions for Managing the "Perfect" Behavioral Interview

1. *Don't be afraid to pause and think through your answer before responding.* While some enthusiasm and animation are helpful, most behavioral interviewers are focused more on the details of your answer than on your nonverbals.

2. *Have in mind an organized format for answering open-ended conversations.* That way, you won't flounder or go off on tangents. The "STAR" structure represents an easy way to help organize your thoughts. It goes like this:

- Briefly describe a *Situation or Task.*
- Explain the *Action* or steps you took.
- Describe the *Results* of your action.

Here's an example of this structure being used during a behavioral interview.

Interviewer: Describe a time you decided to try a different approach to handling a customer problem. What happened?

Applicant: *(Situation)* An irate customer had been sounding off to me for about ten minutes. Even though I had been empathetic and was listening, nothing I could say seemed to calm her down. *(Action)* I knew I had to try something different, so, rather than continuing to explain our position, I reflected her feelings instead. I said, "You really seem upset and angry about what happened."
(Results) What occurred next almost seemed like a miracle. She said, "Yes, I'm damn upset . . ." and went on for another minute venting her anger. Then, almost at once, she relaxed and said, "I know it's not your fault, so let's see how we can solve this problem."

3. *Be prepared for several "negative" questions.* Listed below are three "classics"; you can prepare for them by using Skill Builder 22:

"What was the most difficult problem you had to overcome in your last job? How did you cope with it?"

"Tell me about a time you had difficulty working with a boss or co-worker. How did you handle the situation?"

"Tell me about a difficult decision you had to make. What made it difficult and how did you go about resolving it?"

Situational Interviews

What They're Like

Situational interviews are quite different from the typical face-to-face interview. Instead of conversation, in these interviews you are required to perform a task. These tasks vary, depending upon the technique used.

Situational techniques are often used in conjunction with one-on-one interviews. In some organizations, the situational interview is used for screening; in other companies, you become involved in a situational "test" only if you have first passed muster in your traditional interview.

There are four situational interviews you are most likely to encounter.

Group Problem Solving

In this kind of interview, you might come to your appointment and find yourself placed at one of several tables, each seating three to four other applicants. Someone from the organization addresses the group and tells you that each table represents a "company team" and that each team will have an hour to solve a certain problem. You are told further, that, at your table, the details of the problem and your team's discussion will be facilitated by a company representative (often a consultant or human resources employee).

In-Basket

With this approach you are given a box of memos, telephone messages, appointment schedules, project deadlines, and assorted papers that typically come across a business manager's desk. Your task is to order and prioritize items in a short period of time, usually thirty to forty-five minutes.

Your prospective employers want to observe your organizational skills, thought processes, analytical skills, and ability to handle the stress of time pressure.

Role Play

In a fictitious setting, you are asked to perform a particular task such as making a sales presentation (usually you are given product information and time to prepare). At other times the role play may involve your acting as a consultant, manager, or customer service representative.

During role plays observers try to evaluate your interpersonal skills and ability to handle situations similar to those that will be encountered in the real-life work setting.

Assessment Center

This approach is most often employed when an organization needs to evaluate a large number of candidates for a particular job, that of supervisor, for example. It is more likely to be used for in-house candidates than external applicants.

If you are going to be evaluated by the assessment center method, you will almost always know in advance. One reason is that the evaluation process may span several days.

In most centers, you are likely to encounter a variety of situational interviews, including a mixture of those already cited—in-basket, role plays, and panel interviews. Several observers will rate your performance.

Suggestions for Managing the "Perfect" Situational Interview

The variety and unpredictable nature of these interviews makes it difficult to provide specific recommendations that will consistently produce success. However, the four general principles described here will enhance the likelihood of your success:

1. *Recognize that situational interviews are really performances.* You are "on stage," and therefore your actions will speak louder than words. During group discussions, for example, making a statement that you are a "team player" won't mean much, but your overt display of a cooperative spirit and of give-and-take behavior will definitely be noted.

2. *Learn as much as you can about the prospective employer.* Awareness of its current management philosophies and/or objectives enables you to avoid comments and behavior that may be at cross-purposes with the company's style. For example, "coming on strong" and pushing for your decisions may be highly regarded behavior in some organizations, whereas in others—let's say one that promotes employee empowerment and team decisions—it may be negatively perceived.

3. *In group discussions, try to relax and be yourself.* Above all, be sure to participate. You are likely to make a more positive impression when you allow your natural talents and personality characteristics to unfold than when you attempt to play a role.

4. *Read up on the techniques that situational interviews make use of.* If you know beforehand that you will be involved in a situational interview

(as is likely to be the case with assessment centers) you could do some reading on time management or whatever assignments your networking reveals may be thrown at you. In the final analysis, however, it is you and confidence in your own unique abilities that will carry the day.

SKILL BUILDER 22 Managing Negative Behavioral Questions

Interviewers using the Hypothesis Method or other behavioral interview techniques will often ask ''how'' or ''why'' you reacted to certain events. The ST-A-R formula provides a convenient way to keep your answer on track and to avoid tangents.

I've selected three frequently asked questions as the vehicles for your practice.

Briefly, the ST-A-R formula goes like this:

1. ST = Situations or Task
2. A = Actions you took
3. R = Results attained

Question 1.

What was the most difficult problem you had to overcome in your last job? How did you cope with it?

Situation: Suggestion: Select a problem that is significant; otherwise your positive results won't have much impact. Also, pick a problem that you surmounted by using one or more of your strengths.

One important problem I had to overcome was: ____________________

____

____

____

____

Action: Make it as specific as you can. For example, "I met with my boss and explained exactly what had happened. Then I gave him two recommendations for reducing our department's overtime." Not: "I discussed the situation with my boss."

To solve the problem, I: ______________________________

____

____

____

____

Results: If possible, describe the results in concrete, numerical terms, e.g., ". . . and that reduced our turnover 15 percent."

The end result was: ______________________________

____

____

____

Question 2

Tell me about a time you had difficulty working with a boss or co-worker. How did you handle the situation?

Situation: Suggestion: Don't select a serious relationship issue.

I realized I had a problem when: ______________________________

____

____

____

____

Action:

To solve the problem, I: ______________________________

____

____

Results: Be specific about how the relationship was restored. For example, "My co-worker volunteered to help on the next project."

The end result was: ____________________

Question 3

Tell me about a difficult decision you had to make. What made it difficult and how did you go about resolving it?

Situation: Be sure to answer both questions—what the decision was, and why it was difficult.

A difficult decision I had to make involved: ____________________

Action:

I handled it by: ____________________

Results: ____________________

Chapter 15
Guidelines for Success

This chapter lists a number of suggestions for making the most of your interview opportunity, based on my experience from the "other side of the desk." Each one of these recommendations represents a distinct action that, if taken, will minimize the likelihood of your being rejected. Here they are:

1. *Remember that body language counts.* Be sure to maintain good posture without appearing stiff. Sit in a comfortable position, and curtail any nervous habits (such as running your hand through your hair or playing with your fingers). Try to communicate interest and attentiveness through frequent eye contact.

2. *Speak frankly and confidently.* Focus on your most important accomplishments, but refrain from boasting or exaggerating.

3. *Let your natural personality come through.* Do not try to be somebody you are not. It is extremely difficult to play a role successfully; your interviewer will sense that you "do not ring true." Even if you are successful in fooling the interviewer, you may find yourself in a job for which you really aren't suited.

4. *Consistently project positiveness and enthusiasm.* There may be occasional exceptions to this principle, but it almost always holds true. When the interviewer discusses the company, the job, the challenges, and problems that lie ahead, *overt enthusiasm* is vital. If your attitude isn't positive about these topics during an employment interview, the interviewer will assume that it certainly won't be positive about them at work.

Some applicants who are naturally reticent and controlled experience difficulty in showing enthusiasm. Internally they may feel quite positive and zestful, but you would never know it from simply observing them. If you are one of these people, then it is especially important to outwardly express, using words, the enthusiasm experienced inwardly. Try to make more use of feeling words. For example:

> "I am really *excited* about the challenges on this job."
>
> "I am really feeling *enthusiastic* about all that I've seen thus far."
>
> "I *can't wait* to get started on a project like that!"

Remember, too, that people who appear stiff and controlled can project a more positive image by smiling more often and by emphasizing their thoughts through more frequent use of hand gestures.

5. *Don't be afraid to pause.* Whenever you are confronted with a thought-provoking question, there is no need to try to come up with a quick response. Take your time and think about what you want to say. Pauses of this sort convey a recognition of the importance of the interviewer's question; they also convey a certain amount of self-confidence and maturity. Your pause also avoids the risk of your answers appearing to be canned.

6. *Be open and honest about the negative aspects of your career history.* Instead of denying the obvious, acknowledge the weakness and turn it into an asset. The principle is to show how the limitation has led you to make a positive change or to acquire compensating strengths. Here are a few examples:

> "Yes, I have had a number of job changes in the past, but those experiences have helped me learn what is right for me and what I can best do. The job here is exactly what I want, and I'm now ready to settle down and grow with a company such as yours."

or:

> "It is true that I haven't had extensive experience in that area, but I can tell you I am eager to learn. I also believe that there might be an advantage in my being trained in the way you proceed here. At least, I won't have to unlearn practices that don't fit well here."

or:

> "I have to admit that I react too quickly at times, but I'm aware of that tendency and I'm working on it. The upside is that I can handle a lot of projects at one time and not get rattled."

7. *Don't let the stress interview upset you.* Some interviewers believe it's helpful to see how you handle pressure, so they deliberately create

stress during a portion of the interview. If the interviewer is a hostile person, the entire meeting could become a stress interview. Some typical ways that interviewers create stress are:

- Being silent for extended periods of time.
- Asking you to perform without preparation. For example, the interview might hand you a pencil and say, "Sell me this pencil right now! Convince me to buy it!"
- Asking if you want to smoke, but having no ashtrays in sight.

Hopefully, you will never be exposed to these kinds of strategies; however, if ever you feel pressured, it is important not to let yourself get rattled. This is exactly what most stress interviewers are trying to determine—can you handle the heat?

One effective defense against losing your composure is simply to recognize and accept what is happening. You can say to yourself, "Okay, so he is trying the stress technique. I'm going to stay calm and not get panicked."

Another action that is often helpful is to ask a question about the interviewer's behavior. This needs to be done tactfully, but it usually takes the pressure off by making the interviewer responsible for the next segment of the discussion. You might say, for example:

> "Why are we being silent like this? Is there something you want me to say?"

or:

> "Do you really want me to try to sell you the pencil, or are you just trying to see how I'll react to the stress?"

Each of these seven guidelines is important to keep in mind; failure to put them into action usually results in a turndown—despite an outstanding track record.

One way to learn how well you have applied these concepts is to review this chapter after each interview. Compare your interview experience against each guideline. Skill Builder 24, "Profiting From Your Rehash," provides a helpful format for making this analysis and ensuring your success.

Chapter 16
Concluding the Interview

There is an axiom about selling that states, "Know when the sale is over and then leave." That principle applies equally well to employment interviews. Your interviewer will almost always give an indication when the interview is about to end. It's extremely important to be alert to these signals. Here's one typical indicator that is characteristic, even though it's fairly direct:

> "I think that pretty much covers the ground I wanted to talk about. We have several other candidates that we're looking at, and I'll be getting back to you as soon as we've seen them. We very much appreciate your coming in to see us."

To ignore an obvious closing statement like this and to keep on talking is not only poor judgment but will almost guarantee that you won't get a job offer.

Sometimes an interviewer's cues about terminating the discussion are less direct. For example:

> "All of your comments have been very helpful to me."
>
> "Well, we've certainly covered a lot of ground today."
>
> "I think that pretty well covers it."
>
> "Do you have any other appointments today?"
>
> "We should be getting on now to your next interviewer."

At other times, hints that the interview is over are even more subtle; the cue might only be body language. An interviewer is clearly telling you something if he:

- Peeks at his watch or wall clock.
- Begins shuffling papers on his desk.
- Glances at his appointment calendar.

Whatever the cues—subtle or direct—it is not prudent to ignore them. The more straightforward they are, the more essential it is to react to them. When the interviewer's remarks are unequivocal, as in the first example, you should begin your closing (strategies for closing are discussed at the end of this chapter).

On the other hand, sometimes the words or body language are so subtle that it may be worthwhile to check out your perceptions. Rarely is anything gained by prematurely terminating an interview. You could say something like this:

> "I couldn't help noticing your glancing at the clock. Is our time just about up?"

It is always acceptable to check expectations. You could say, for instance:

> "How are we doing with your time? Do we have much left?"

or:

> "Do we still have a few minutes? There are a couple of questions I would like to ask."

Whether you now proceed with the interview or move to your closing depends, of course, on the interviewer's response. Unless his comments strongly suggest that he wants to continue, you should realize that it is time to pack up and say goodbye.

When to Keep the Interview Going

There are times when it is important to make an effort at keeping the interview going, even though the interviewer has given a signal that it's going to end. For example:

- You believe that the interviewer misunderstood something you said earlier in the interview, and you want to clarify your statement.
- Your interviewer gave you a clue about an important requirement for the job, and you have some meaningful, related information about your background that was not mentioned earlier.

In these cases, tactfully request time to continue. You could say something like this:

> "I realize that it's time to end this interview, but do you have a moment for me to make one additional comment about . . . ? I think you will find it helpful to you."

If the interviewer does not seem receptive to your request, you always have the option of providing additional data in a letter or telephone conversation. However, information supplied after the interview rarely has the same impact as something conveyed during the interview itself.

Occasionally, on your trip home or on the following day, you think of something you left out or should have said during your interview. In these instances, a telephone call is the preferred remedy; it's quicker than a letter, and, even more important, it gives you another exposure to the interviewer—a second chance to sell yourself.

It's Never Over Until It's Over

The interview is not over until you have a letter extending an offer or telling you that you're rejected. Until either one of these events takes place, you are still a candidate. Don't let your guard down and jeopardize a highly favorable impression by saying the wrong thing in a situation you deem to be harmless.

One of the partners in a large public accounting firm shared with me an interview process that he claims has saved him from making many serious hiring mistakes. Once an applicant passes through his organization's beauty parade and has been judged acceptable, he invites the candidate to dinner. The candidate very likely senses that she did well in all of the interviews; she "knows" that the partner would not bother with this "let's get acquainted" dinner if she were not going to be made an offer.

The partner deliberately chooses a relaxing, comfortable restaurant, not a stuffy one. He keeps the conversation light, sharing some personal aspects of his own life and encouraging the candidate to do so as well. From the applicant's perspective, it's a warm way of being welcomed into the firm.

What the applicant doesn't realize is that she is definitely being interviewed. The partner is listening carefully for attitudes about travel—about being away from home and family a significant portion of most workweeks. He is listening for the applicant's assessment of her spouse's support for this kind of away-from-home life-style.

The partner told me that he has long since learned that if an employee's family is not supportive of extended absences from home, the chances of the firm recouping its substantial investment in the training of that employee are not good. If the candidate, in a moment of relaxed camaraderie, mentions problems at home that need her attention (or any other pressures that might restrict travel), what seemed to be a celebration dinner will end up being the reason for her rejection.

The point of all this is that *anyone in any way connected to your prospective employer has the potential for killing a job offer—no matter how innocuous he may seem.* You are always an interviewee until you have the offer in your pocket.

Sneaky? Yes. But the corporate world is replete with stories of similar tricks of the trade. The best defense is being forewarned.

Closing the Interview *Your* Way

Let's assume now that you've said all that you want to say, and the interviewer indicates that the meeting is over. At this point you may feel relieved and want to say "thank you" and go. But often it's to your advantage to end on a different note. Whether this next suggestion is appropriate or not will depend on the circumstances and the level of job you are seeking. The idea is to keep yourself in a proactive mode rather than a passive one. You might say something like this:

> "I'm going to be in and out much of the time during the next week or two, so you may have difficulty in reaching me. I am very interested in this job, so would it be all right if I called you next week to see if you've made a decision?"

Regardless of whether or not you adopt a proactive stance, there are three important core concepts that you should include in your exit statement:

1. Your strong interest in the position
2. Your excitement and enthusiasm about the job/company
3. Your confidence in your ability to do the job

Here's an example:

> "Thank you so much for your time today, Mrs. Jones. After all that I've heard, I'm really excited about this job. I know that my sales experience and drive will help me get on board and be productive very quickly. I'll be looking forward to your decision and, hopefully, to seeing you again.

You want to leave the interviewer reassured that his decision to make you an offer is the right one. This means that it is as important to pay attention to your exit as it is to your entrance. Folding up and quietly slipping away at the end can easily undermine a good impression made during your interview. For this reason it is a good idea to plan and rehearse your basic exit statement. Naturally, it will need to be altered for each different interview situation, but the three core concepts listed should always be embedded in what you say.

To help prepare your exit statement, try Skill Builder 23 at the end of the chapter.

One Final Action

On your way out (if you haven't done so already), see if you can get the name of your interviewer's secretary. If you plan on calling your interviewer later, it makes such a difference when you are able to say, "Is this Celine? I was in last week talking with Mr. Dillon and . . . ."

Skill Builder 23
Preparing Your Exit Statement

It may not be good practice to memorize your exit statement because it will need to be adjusted to fit each circumstance. However, all exit statements should try to convey three major points:

1. Your strong interest in the position
2. Your excitement and enthusiasm about the job/company
3. Your confidence in your ability to do the job

In the following spaces, try to design a generalized exit statement that you can revise to fit each situation.

1. A "thank you" in words that are natural and comfortable for you:

____

____

2. Some words that you can comfortably use to express enthusiasm or excitement about the job and/or company:

____

____

3. Some specific skills, traits, or experiences that convey your confidence in your ability to do the job:

____

____

4. A socially polite way to say "goodbye." Again, use words that come comfortably and naturally. You shouldn't have to think about how to phrase this portion of your exit statement.

____

____

It might be helpful now to consolidate the sections above into one smooth, integrated statement. Writing it out one more time will help reinforce the three important exit statement concepts. Then, at the end of your next interview, your positive impact will be enhanced.

____

____

____

____

____

____

____

If you needed more space than that provided, your statement is probably too long. It should not be a speech; it's only a closing comment.

Section Four

After the Interview

Chapter 17
The Rehash

As soon as you leave the interview, you are likely to begin mentally rehashing what occurred—consciously or unconsciously. It's hard to avoid second-guessing yourself, wondering, "Should I have said more about this? Less about that? What about my answer to the salary question?" If you wanted the job, the self-questioning is almost inevitable. But that's okay. It's a valuable exercise to engage in. Just as a sports team views films of its previous game to learn about mistakes made, as well as to analyze good performances, so you can use this rehash as an opportunity to improve your interviewing skills. A few suggested items to incorporate into your rehash are:

1. *Review what went well and what didn't go so well.* Understanding these two aspects of the interview is critical. Careful analysis of your past performance can significantly improve your effectiveness during your next interview. You'll know better what to highlight and what to play down.

While it may seem to be a nuisance, I strongly recommend writing out your observations on the Company Fact Sheet. The discipline of writing usually helps us to better get our thoughts in order, and to take a deeper look at events, than if we simply mull them over in our minds. This is especially helpful when the interview results are negative.

Writing out your reactions is an excellent way of discharging negative feelings and getting them off your chest; discouraged feelings won't drag you down so much. Also, if you are working with an outplacement firm, you may find it quite productive to review these notes with your counselor; they could provide the focus for a few practice interviews.

Some questions to consider in your rehash are:

- What things about myself (talents, experiences, traits) did the interviewer react favorably to?
- What did I say about myself that did not seem to make a favorable impression on my interviewer?
- What appealed to me about the job? The organization?

- What did I hear about the job/organization that was not appealing?
- If I could do the interview over, what, if anything, would I do differently?
- What is the best next step for me to take now with regard to this job opportunity?

To help you conduct your rehash after each interview, use Skill Builder 24. It provides a practical worksheet for organizing your thoughts.

2. *Record names.* This is especially important if you were interviewed by several individuals. It is most valuable if you can write down a brief comment about each interviewer's:

- Role in the organization
- Priorities—what was important to this person
- Reactions to you—what he seemed to like and dislike

This information could be very useful in any subsequent discussions with these individuals or others in the firm.

3. *Complete next steps.* If you are interviewing several companies, it is easy to slip up on important follow-through items. For example, perhaps during the interview you were asked to name some references, and you want to prepare these people for the forthcoming reference call. Jotting down a reminder to alert them is the best way to ensure that the necessary calls are not overlooked. Another typical item that's helpful to write about is any commitment you may have made to your interviewer, such as sending supplementary materials or calling in on a particular date.

To make your rehash most productive, jot down your important conclusions on your Company Fact Sheet at the soonest possible moment.

Rehash After a Bad Interview

Let's say you have just come from an interview that clearly did not go well. Let's further assume that you very much wanted the job. Rehashes after such interviews have the potential to be real downers. But they needn't be so.

First of all, writing out your reactions on the Company Fact Sheet or on Skill Builder 24 can be quite cathartic. It's a great way to get rid of your negative feelings. Second, it's helpful to recall that it is impossible to please everyone. No matter who you are—no matter how talented, socially skillful, friendly, and intelligent—someone may not like you or may be threatened by you. What is done is done. Consider the failure an opportunity to learn, and start focusing on your next interview.

Rehash After a Good (or Even So-So) Interview

Much can be learned after a good interview. If you complete the Skill Builder, you will have cataloged those of your comments that made a good impression. Even if you accept an offer, such information will be useful for future interviews, which sometimes come up more quickly than you anticipate. For example, once you're on the job, an in-house opening may occur for which you are a candidate. The know-how derived from your rehash will be just as useful as you interview within the organization as it was when you applied for the job in the company in the first place.

It should be noted, too, that after a "good interview," you'll feel a strong tendency to relax. Sometimes you gain such an increase in self-esteem and confidence that you rest in your job-seeking efforts. In my outplacement counseling, I have often observed men and women cancel interview appointments because they believed that they were sure to get an offer. There were many who were deeply saddened when no offer came.

It is important to keep the job pursuit active—good interviews or not. Momentum is important; keep it going.

SKILL BUILDER 24
Profiting From Your Rehash

Now that your first interview is over, writing about your observations can help you become even more successful in your next one. This Skill Builder represents an excellent way to debrief yourself after each interview.

Interview 1

Interview Date: ____/____/____

Name of Company: ______________________________

Name of Interviewer: ______________________________

Title: ______________________________

Name of Secretary: ______________________________

The Interviewer's Reactions

The interviewer seemed favorably impressed by my [talents/experience/traits/attitude]. Be specific:

1. ______________________________
2. ______________________________
3. ______________________________

Some things I said or did that did *not* seem to favorably impress the interviewer were:

1. ______________________________
2. ______________________________
3. ______________________________

Your Impressions

What appealed to me about the job/organization (authority, pay, opportunities to learn, advancement)?

1. ______________________________
2. ______________________________
3. ______________________________

What aspects of the organization were least appealing?

1. ______________________________
2. ______________________________
3. ______________________________

Considering my experiences during this interview, what have I learned that I can use during the next one?______________________________

____

____

____

What can I do, specifically, to make my next interview even more effective?

1. ____

____

____

2. ____

____

____

Next, consider reviewing this Skill Builder with a friend, outplacement counselor, or executive recruiter. These individuals may help you interpret the situation more clearly and may have constructive suggestions for improvement. If you judged your interview to be successful, rehashing it with your recruiter (assuming you are working with one) might add to his confidence in you as a marketable prospect.

Use one of these Skill Builders after each interview. Relevant segments of your responses can be transferred to your Company Fact Sheet.

Profiting From Your Rehash—Interview 2

Interview Date: _____/_____/_____

Name of Company: ____

Name of Interviewer: ____

Title: ____

Name of Secretary: ____

The Interviewer's Reactions

The interviewer seemed favorably impressed by my [talents, experiences, traits, attitude]. *Be specific:*

1. ____
2. ____
3. ____

Some things I said or actions I took that did *not* seem to favorably impress the interviewer were:

1. ______________________________
2. ______________________________
3. ______________________________

Your Impressions

What appealed to me about the job/organization (authority, pay, opportunities to learn, advancement)?

1. ______________________________
2. ______________________________
3. ______________________________

What aspects of the organization were least appealing:

1. ______________________________
2. ______________________________
3. ______________________________

Considering my experiences during this interview, what have I learned that I can use during the next one?______________________________

____

____

____

What can I do, specifically, to make my next interview even more effective:

1. ______________________________

____

2. ______________________________

____

Transfer relevant portions of this Skill Builder to the Company Fact Sheet for this organization.

Profiting From Your Rehash—Interview 3

Interview Date: ____/____/____

Name of Company: ______________________________

Name of Interviewer: ______________________________

Title: ______________________________

Name of Secretary: ______________________________

The Interviewer's Reactions

The interviewer seemed favorably impressed by my [talents, experiences, traits, attitude]. *Be specific:*

1. ______________________________
2. ______________________________
3. ______________________________

Some things I said or actions I took that did *not* seem to favorably impress the interviewer were:

1. ______________________________
2. ______________________________
3. ______________________________

Your Impressions

What appealed to me about the job/organization (authority, pay, opportunities to learn, advancement)?

1. ______________________________
2. ______________________________
3. ______________________________

What aspects of the organization were least appealing?

1. ______________________________
2. ______________________________
3. ______________________________

Considering my experiences during this interview, what have I learned that I can use during the next one?____________________

____

____

____

What can I do, specifically, to make my next interview even more effective?

1. ____________________________________
   ____
2. ____________________________________
   ____

Transfer relevant portions of this Skill Builder to the Company Fact Sheet for this organization.

Profiting From Your Rehash—Interview 4

Interview Date: ____/____/____

Name of Company: ____________________________

Name of Interviewer: ____________________________

Title: ____________________________________

Name of Secretary: ____________________________

The Interviewer's Reactions

The interviewer seemed favorably impressed by my [talents, experiences, traits, attitude]. *Be specific:*

1. ____________________________________
2. ____________________________________
3. ____________________________________

Some things I said or actions I took that did *not* seem to favorably impress the interviewer were:

1. __________
2. __________
3. __________

Your Impressions

What appealed to me about the job/organization (authority, pay, opportunities to learn, advancement)?

1. __________
2. __________
3. __________

What aspects of the organization were least appealing?

1. __________
2. __________
3. __________

Considering my experiences during this interview, what have I learned that I can use during the next one? __________

____

____

____

What can I do, specifically, to make my next interview even more effective?

1. __________
   ____
2. __________
   ____

Transfer relevant portions of this Skill Builder to the Company Fact Sheet for this organization.

Profiting From Your Rehash—Interview 5

Interview Date: ____/____/____

Name of Company: ____________________

Name of Interviewer: ____________________

Title: ____________________

Name of Secretary: ____________________

The Interviewer's Reactions

The interviewer seemed favorably impressed by my [talents, experiences, traits, attitude]. *Be specific:*

1. ____________________
2. ____________________
3. ____________________

Some things I said or actions I took that did *not* seem to favorably impress the interviewer were:

1. ____________________
2. ____________________
3. ____________________

Your Impressions

What appealed to me about the job/organization (authority, pay, opportunities to learn, advancement)?

1. ____________________
2. ____________________
3. ____________________

What aspects of the organization were least appealing?

1. ____________________
2. ____________________
3. ____________________

Considering my experiences during this interview, what have I learned that I can use during the next one? ______________________

____

____

____

What can I do, specifically, to make my next interview even more effective?

1. ______________________________________

____

2. ______________________________________

____

Transfer relevant portions of this Skill Builder to the Company Fact Sheet for this organization.

Profiting From Your Rehash—Interview 6

Interview Date: ____/____/____

Name of Company: ______________________________

Name of Interviewer: ______________________________

Title: ______________________________

Name of Secretary: ______________________________

The Interviewer's Reactions

The interviewer seemed favorably impressed by my [talents, experiences, traits, attitude]. *Be specific:*

1. ______________________________________
2. ______________________________________
3. ______________________________________

Some things I said or actions I took that did *not* seem to favorably impress the interviewer were:

1. ______________________________
2. ______________________________
3. ______________________________

Your Impressions

What appealed to me about the job/organization (authority, pay, opportunities to learn, advancement)?

1. ______________________________
2. ______________________________
3. ______________________________

What aspects of the organization were least appealing?

1. ______________________________
2. ______________________________
3. ______________________________

Considering my experiences during this interview, what have I learned that I can use during the next one? ______________________________

____

____

____

What can I do, specifically, to make my next interview even more effective?

1. ______________________________

   ____

2. ______________________________

   ____

Transfer relevant portions of this Skill Builder to the Company Fact Sheet for this organization.

Chapter 18

If You Get an Offer/ If You Don't Get an Offer

Handling the aftermath of a series of interviews, whether or not you actually receive a job offer, can require some difficult decisions and can stir up some deep-seated emotions. Whichever way the company decides, there are certain steps you can take to ease the process.

If You Get an Offer: Deciding Yes or No

Whether deciding to accept a job offer is difficult or easy depends, of course, on the attractiveness of the offer and how badly you want the job. It may well be that you are going to accept any reasonable offer because financial, psychological, or family needs so dictate. In such cases, you can skip over this section.

But suppose the decision is not that clear-cut. Maybe you have more than one offer; maybe the job, while a good one, isn't exactly what you initially had in mind. How can you decide?

Here are five questions that can help you make the right decision:

1. *Can you do the job?* Is this a job you can succeed in? Will your education and experience enable you to really make a contribution? If you believe you can do it and feel good about your ability to be successful, then give yourself a "yes" to this question.

2. *Do you like the people?* Are these the kind of individuals you enjoy being with? Did one or more turn you off? (This is especially important if you will be working directly for these particular individuals). Was the atmosphere comfortable for you? Remember, during the interview, these people were on their best behavior. If certain individuals annoyed you, the annoyance won't be diminished once you're on board. If you liked the people you met—if they're your kind of people—then answer "yes" to this question.

3. *Do they need you?* This is an important question. Even if you can do this job and you like the people, that's not enough. The issue here is, are you the right fit? Are you the kind of person the company needs in this particular job?

For example, suppose that your interviewers described the prior incumbent in the job for which you are being interviewed as disorganized and unable to control expenses, with the result that the operation was run in too loose a fashion. The strong implication of these statements is that the company is looking for someone with strong administrative skills who will run a tight ship. If implementing strong controls is one of your strengths, then the company needs someone like you. On the other hand, if running a tight ship is not your style, the match may not be good; each of you could easily become disenchanted with the other in the early stages of your employment.

4. *Do your values match?* Every organization has a distinctive personality. Some are easy to sense, even after a brief exposure; sometimes you get a feel for the organization's temperament the minute you walk into the reception room. For example, in some organizations you might observe a bare-bones room, functional furniture, and no decorative frills (such as flowers or artwork). The company might strike you as being practical and frugal—one which places more value on getting the job done than on sensitivity toward its employees or visitors.

If there is a mismatch between your values and those of the company, the likely result will be dissatisfaction. It may not occur immediately after you start the job, but sooner or later you will likely discover that you are experiencing the feeling that something is wrong.

Suppose, for instance, that you are family-oriented—that having time for spouse and children is an important value for you. You like to be free during most evenings and on weekends to help the children with their homework and to play with them; you have a close relationship with your spouse and enjoy spending time together. If you join a company whose value system includes an "up or out" philosophy, where almost everyone is striving to look good and get ahead, where long hours are traditional and expected, then the eventual conflict between the two value systems will begin taking its toll. Either you will begin changing your values or you will start looking for ways to extricate yourself from the organization.

After a recent telephone survey conducted by *USA Today*, the editors summarized their findings with the headlines, "Callers Want Work to Fit Needs, Values." A majority of the respondents were clearly unhappy about the differences between their expectations and those of the company they worked for. If quality of life is a concern to you, then it is important to compare your values with those of the organization you are considering joining.

Sometimes it is difficult to get a fix on a company's values. Many organizations have published value statements; however, the way life is lived in the company is often quite different from the professed values! The best way to find out what the lived values really are is to ask your interviewers, and others who may intimately know the company, this question: "What is it like to work here?" Listen carefully, and don't hurry your speaker; the last few comments may be more revealing than the beginning remarks.

Before you can determine if the company is right for you, you will need a clear understanding of your own values. Unfortunately, they are not always easy to determine. People often have competing values, so the solution is to set priorities. Skill Builder 25 may help you identify values that you should consider in making a job choice.

5. *Do the job, location, values, and people feel right?* When all is said and done, what is your gut feeling? Taking a job has something in common with buying a car, a boat, or a house. While you might carefully weigh all the facts of the situation, when it comes right down to the final decision, it's what you feel in your heart that tips the scale. I believe it's the same with a new job. If you don't feel highly positive, with a sense of excitement about your new job opportunity, it probably isn't right for you. You receive many subliminal cues during any employment interview process, so whatever vibes you are experiencing are real, even though you can't put your finger on the source.

If you said yes to questions 1 through 4, but you are not experiencing positive vibes, take a hard look at the opportunity before you accept the offer. One helpful technique is to try to identify the source of the negative feelings. Once you do this, you can determine how significant the factor is, as well as the possibility of rectifying it. Usually, the reaction stems not so much from what was said during the interviews but how it was said. Look for the source of your vibes in certain attitudes that might have been conveyed.

If your answer to each of the five questions is positive, then go for it! The job offered is very likely to be the right one for you.

The "Cold Feet" Phenomenon

Sometimes a few negatives in a new job situation make the whole opportunity look black. It's helpful to remember that no job is ideal—all have pluses and minuses. If the key issues (the five questions, just described) are satisfactory, the odds are good that the job will work out.

If You Don't Get an Offer

Not getting an offer for a job you wanted can be devastating. Much of most people's sense of self-worth is tied to success at work, and you could easily judge the absence of an offer as a failure. Even more pertinent are the feelings of rejection; you put your best foot forward, yet it appears that you were not acceptable. But please note, all of these negative conclusions are simply your perception of the situation. The reality of the situation is that you are still the same capable person that you were before and that what appeared to be rejection of you as a person may be nothing of the sort.

There is absolutely nothing wrong with having feelings of sadness, anxiety, anger, fear, or discouragement. Feelings happen spontaneously; you don't choose to have them or not to have them. As a consequence, feelings are neither right nor wrong—they just are. They are a wonderful part of our human make-up. It is important, however, to understand the importance of these feelings as they relate to your "no-offer" situation. Here are two key points:

1. *Feelings control behavior.* If you feel angry, eventually those feelings will manifest themselves in how you act. You may be irritable, have an outburst of temper, or become moody or depressed. If someone hurts your feelings, you won't be warm and cordial but will be more likely to act aloof and distant. And so it is with your job-hunting situation. Your sense of failure or rejection may lead to feelings of discouragement. These feelings could result in your behaving in a less confident or enthusiastic manner in your next interview; at the worst, you could become so depressed that you find it difficult to mobilize yourself for another interview.

2. *Feelings derive from your perception of the situation.* The kinds of feelings experienced when you get turned down for a job depend upon what you believe actually happened—on your perceptions. These perceptions, in turn, are shaped by your self-image. The important point is that your perceptions of the turndown are less likely to lead to negative feelings if you have an educated and objective view of the employment scene.

It's a good idea to consider the following realities of the job marketplace:

- For many jobs—especially those advertised—employers may obtain four hundred or more résumés and interview twenty or more people for each position. When you think about it, the odds of getting a job offer are very slim.

- Even if you were qualified and interviewed well, you may not get an offer because:
  —The company changed its mind about filling the vacancy.
  —The company changed its mind about the qualifications it wanted in the hiree.
  —You looked great, but internal company politics led to a decision to fill the job from within.
  —You looked great, but a friend of one of the company executives got the nod.
  —You looked great, but someone else had more experience or know-how in an area the company deemed to be important.
  —You looked great but your minimum salary requirements were more than the company was willing to pay.

For the six reasons just mentioned, there are probably six more that you couldn't even imagine. Furthermore, the company is not likely to tell you the actual reason for a turndown—it will simply tell you that it selected someone else who was "more qualified." When you think of the odds against getting an offer, it doesn't seem to make much sense agonizing over why you didn't get it. The more realistic expectation is that you won't get an offer.

When you've lost out on a job you wanted, there are three constructive steps you can take to get yourself back on track and help turn a potentially negative experience into one that you can learn and profit from.

What to Do When You Get a Turndown

1. *Do the "rehashing" as suggested in Chapter 17.* You may not have received the offer because of something you said or did that is correctable.

2. *Examine how you feel.* If your feelings are negative, try to determine the roots of the feelings. In other words, what judgments have you made that produced the feelings? How justified are your judgments? Are other, less self-damaging explanations equally probable? Awareness that the turndown may have been completely unrelated to you or your qualifications may result in more constructive reactions. Sometimes listening to well-intended advice from friends can help you gain a new perspective on what happened.

3. *If negative feelings still persist, talk them out.* One way to be free from being controlled by your feelings is to express your feelings to people—spouse, friend, or outplacement counselor. Ask them to listen to you for a moment, say that you need to get something off your chest. Then describe to them the emotions you are experiencing. If you're feeling down, for example, do you feel as though you'd like to cry, or is it more a feeling

of mild disappointment such as you feel when a restaurant doesn't have available the one item on the menu that you wanted? If you still feel depressed, talking with a psychiatrist or psychologist could be most helpful.

By talking out your feelings, you will free yourself to renew your efforts to pursue the job you want.

SKILL BUILDER 25
Clarifying Your Values

It may be helpful to distinguish values from desires. Values are deep-rooted; they impact on your behavior. Desires are surface wishes and are not always acted upon. I may, for example, desire long vacations but stay in a job that does not provide them. If I value time with my family, I will tolerate a job that makes me work on weekends only until I can get something else.

One way to get in touch with your values is to list them in order of priority. Listed are a number of values that can be related to a career choice. Read this list carefully, and then try to identify those that are most and least important to you. Be brutally honest with yourself:

1. Job security
2. High income
3. Time for family
4. Cordial co-workers
5. Geographic location
6. Opportunity for advancement
7. Geographical stability
8. Working with those who share my spiritual values
9. Independence/autonomy
10. Service to others
11. Variety of tasks
12. Prestige/status
13. Opportunity for creative expression
14. Working with those who share my ethical values
15. Adventure/travel
16. Other____

Now, try to select from the list the six most important and six least important. Once you've written them in the spaces, try to rank-order your most important values by placing a 1 next to the item that is your strongest value, a 2 next to the second strongest, and so on.

My Six Most Important Values

Value	*Priority Rank*
______________________________	________
______________________________	________
______________________________	________
______________________________	________
______________________________	________
______________________________	________

My Six Least Important Values

Value	*Priority Rank*
______________________________	________
______________________________	________
______________________________	________
______________________________	________
______________________________	________
______________________________	________

As you examine your highest and lowest priorities, decide what must be present in the job or organization that will match your values.

"The job/organization should allow me to ______________________________

____

____

____

____

____"

Chapter 19

Should You Negotiate the Comp?

"What am I going to get?" It's such an important question that the answer cannot be left to evolve haphazardly. Unless your job offer is one that rewards you so handsomely that you just can't refuse, some negotiating is appropriate and even expected.

But before you start negotiating, don't forget everything is not signed, sealed, and delivered yet. You are still an applicant, and you are still being evaluated. You need to be careful not to mess up a successful employment interview by appearing too aggressive during negotiations. It is easy for this to happen if you listen to well-intended advice from friends. If you've been a warm, friendly individual during all of your interviews and you then receive an offer, the company is probably quite satisfied with your cordial, pleasant make-up. Should you suddenly change to a hard-nosed, tough-minded negotiator, you may end up not being hired at all. *Please remember that negotiations are still part of the interview process; you are still being judged.* Everything that has been said earlier about taking cues from the interviewer, being a good listener, and not oververbalizing still applies.

Negotiation Strategies

Almost all negotiations begin from your current earnings. This amount represents the base from which you can expect your income to increase. In almost all hiring situations, prospective employers will expect that you will want more than your present earnings. The issue is, how much more? Even if you are unemployed, from the employer's perspective the expectation is that you will not want to regress to a salary lower than that you have previously earned.

If you have not worked before and this will be your first job, then obviously there is little basis for negotiation. In these instances you want a competitive salary, but consideration of your acceptance zone (see Chapter 6) will help in talking about your compensation expectations.

Since current earnings usually provide the starting point for whatever negotiations you embark on, it's very important to have a good fix on this number. Your current earnings should include cash (base salary or commissions) plus the value of other benefits; after all, they are all part of your compensation. This is not a figure that should be "guesstimated." It needs to be a solid number that will stand up to scrutiny now and in future discussions. If you are working with an executive recruiter, for example, one of the first questions you'll be asked is, "What are your earnings?" It is this figure, more than any other factor, that usually determines how much further that discussion will go.

If the prospective employer believes you have a good deal where you are now, then the company may well present an offer that will be attractive, considering all that you currently have going for you. Thus, it is smart to be clear, right up front, as to the amount of your present compensation.

This is as good a time as any to start figuring out your compensation by completing Skill Builder 26, at the end of this chapter.

Using Your Compensation Data

The purpose of completing Skill Builder 26 is to arrive at your compensation figure. It is not a table of calculations that you drop into your interviewer's lap. The result is something you use to answer the question: "What's your current compensation? A typical response might be:

> "Well, last year my total compensation was $75,000, but in the coming fiscal year, it's very likely to be in the neighborhood of $90,000."

Sometimes, because company profits are down, incentive compensation and bonuses might be lower in the current year than they were in the preceding year, when company earnings were better. In such instances there is no problem with stating two years' earnings:

> "For the past two years my total compensation has run between $55,000 and $80,000."

Please note that I have not included in the compensation list the value of classic fringe benefits such as medical and life insurance. These are competitive in most medium-to-large organizations, and if you added them to your list of compensation, it would appear as though you were trying too hard to inflate the compensation total. However, if you have some extraordinary fringe, like a million-dollar insurance package that covers home, car, and travel, that would be worth including.

Should You Hand Out Your Compensation Figuring?

I want to say, "Definitely not," because it would look as though you were too preoccupied with rewards or money; you do this analysis primarily to be certain that you've computed the right number. But if an executive recruiter or potential employer asks how you arrived at your compensation figure, you could provide an informal work-up. *Don't* have it typed or make it look like a presentation. Once again, that might create the wrong impression. Simply have a neatly outlined, penned listing of your various and expected compensations.

In brief, wherever possible, let your current rewards do the talking for you. Negotiation is always risky; help your prospective employer recognize that you have a good thing going right now and that it's going to take more than what you are currently making to pry you away. If you can accomplish this, the odds are in your favor that the offer will be quite attractive.

SKILL BUILDER 26
Figuring Your Total Compensation

To complete this exercise, all you need to do is fill in the blank spaces. Note how impending earnings are also included.

	Current (19__)	*Impending (19__)*
Base salary	____________	____________
Commissions	____________	____________
Bonus	____________	____________
Incentives (cash or deferred)	____________	____________
Stock options (annualized value)	____________	____________
Value of other "perks":		

	(current)	(impending)
memberships	______	______
car allowance	______	______
other	______	______
TOTAL	______	______

Section Five
Concluding Comments

Chapter 20

Be Yourself

When all is said and done, whether you get a job offer or not depends on how much the interviewers liked you. Of course, your qualifications to do the job are important, but remember that, in most instances, you were invited to the interview because someone had already reviewed your background and decided that you would be worth talking with. Once you are in the interview, it's less a matter of convincing your interviewers that you can do the job than of convincing them that you are the kind of person they want in the job.

Four Key Points

This book is filled with recommendations and suggestions for enhancing your ability to present yourself favorably. I hope each of the ideas will help you in some way. But if I were pressed to select the four most important behaviors to concentrate on, I would choose these:

1. Don't oververbalize—be brief and to the point.
2. Be enthusiastic—exhibit energy and vitality.
3. Be positive—express overtly that you like what you see.
4. Know your skills and strengths and express them with confidence.

Saying too much, being a "bump on a log," and reacting in a less than positive way are the behaviors that result in most applicants' failing to get a job offer. Being positive is especially important because it is easy to slip up on. Even before the interview, it is helpful to review whatever negative vibes you may have about the company, industry, or location and prepare yourself to see all of these in as positive a light as possible.

Suppose, for example, you're a New Englander; your roots and friends are all there. You have been invited for an interview with a firm in Chicago, and your initial reaction is negative—you don't like life in the big cities, and the Midwest is certainly not New England. Given this mind-set about the job location, how will you respond when the interviewer asks, "How do you feel about relocating to Chicago?" If you don't prepare yourself to be positive, your answer could cast a shadow over other, more convincing aspects of your interview.

To deal with this problem, you begin to think of all the *upside aspects* of your relocating to Chicago. You like to sail—you'll be right on Lake Michigan; your sister lives in Peoria, Illinois—it will be easy to visit her; you'd like to work on an MBA—Chicago has a number of good graduate schools that offer evening MBA programs. The point is that you not only need to be positive about the job and the location; *what you say must be convincing.* It means a lot more when you provide a few good reasons why Chicago is appealing than if you simply say, "Chicago is fine; I don't have any problems in relocating here."

On Being Honest

When interviewing, people often have a tendency to gloss over weaknesses and exaggerate strengths and accomplishments. It's natural; you're trying to make the most impressive showing you can. No one expects you to talk yourself down or highlight your limitations. But there is a clear difference between your *opinion* about your ability to manage a staff of twenty-five and the *fact* of whether you ever managed a group of that size.

Never lie. Whatever the temptation, no matter how small the issue, it is always a bad decision. First of all, it is dishonest. Second, it is almost impossible to lie consistently. Interviewers are constantly looking for inconsistencies between what you say, your résumé, and comments from references. Nothing turns off a prospective employer more than finding that she has been deceived or that you've misrepresented yourself. How could she possibly trust you as an employee?

If you are asked a factual question such as, "Did you graduate?" "Did you originate that particular design?" or "Were you let go?" be honest. There is merit in candor. If you are forthright and honest about difficult or sensitive issues, you will almost surely command respect from the interviewer. She will certainly feel trusting of you. And while your specific answer may not be the favorable one the interviewer was looking for, the total impact of your presentation will be positive. Let's look at an example:

Interviewer: [*referring to a prior job*]: Were you let go?

Applicant: Frankly, yes. As you may know, a whole new management team took over our division, and my new

> boss brought his own staff with him. I could have stayed, but in a job that really didn't appeal to me.

The above answer is candid, yet brief. Long explanations or skirting around the fact only create suspicion and distrust.

Much has been said in this book about what to say and how to say it. The advice is predicated on years of experience in interviewing and training applicants. However, *to ring true, you must be yourself and not play a role. This means that you need to believe in your own goodness.* Each of you, in your own unique way, has traits and abilities that make you good and effective—it's this goodness that needs to be portrayed, not whatever person you think you should be.

Well, then, what about all the suggestions made in this text? Most of the recommendations are strategies and procedures—they do not directly affect who you are. Other recommendations, however, suggest modifications in behavior. This is the issue in question. You can build on the true you, make minor modifications in external behavior, and still be yourself. Enthusiasm is a good example. If you tend to be stiff and unexpressive, it would be out of character to engage in extensive handwaving and to use many emotion-laden adjectives. But *some* use of hands, *some* effort to smile a little more, and *some* enthusiasm in tone of voice are all possible without coming across as phony. These capabilities are already present in your make-up. They simply need to be freed up.

Please remember: *Small changes in your behavior can have a significantly bigger impact in interpersonal relationships.* You don't have to alter your behavior much for it to have a big impact.

Chapter 21
Good Wishes

We have finally come to the end of our journey together, and I want to extend a personal wish for success in your job search. I hope this book has enabled you to put forth the best of you. There is always a job that's just right for who you are. If you search hard enough and help your interviewers get to know you, career success will follow.

If there is some aspect of interviewing that you want to know more about or if you have an experience that would be helpful to other applicants, I would like to include it in the next edition of *The Perfect Interview.* If your comments are used, I will send you a complimentary copy of the new book. Please write to me care of the publisher: AMACOM Books, 1601 Broadway, New York, NY 10019.

I look forward to hearing from you.

Sources

Cover Letter and Résumés

Adams Publishing. *The Adams Cover Letters.* Holbrook, Mass.: Adams Publishing, 1995.
Beatty, Richard. *The Résumé Kit.* New York: John Wiley, 1990.
Eyler, David. *Résumés That Mean Business.* New York: Random House, 1996.
Fry, Ron. *Your First Résumé.* Franklin Lakes, N.J.: Career Press, 1996.
Jackson, Tom. *The Perfect Résumé.* New York: Doubleday, 1990.
Lucht, John. *Executive Job Changing Workbook.* New York: Viceroy Press, 1994.
Morin, Laura. *Every Woman's Essential Job Hunting & Résumé Book.* Holbrook, Mass.: Bob Adams, Inc., 1994.
Reed, Jean. *Résumés That Get Jobs.* New York: Simon & Schuster, 1995.

Directories

Directory of Corporate Affiliations. National Register Publishing Company, a division of Reed Reference Publishing, P. O. Box 31, New Providence, N.J. 07974. Volume I and II, *U.S. Public* (3,000+ pages); Volume III, *U.S. Private* (2,000+ pages). Lists divisions and subdivisions of public and private companies.
Directory of Executive Recruiters. Kennedy Publications, Fitzwilliams, N.H. 03447. A comprehensive listing of both retainer and contingency firms along with names of one or more staff members.
Directory of Leading Private Companies. Reed Reference Publishing, P.O. Box 31, New Providence, N.J. 07974. Profiles 22,000 companies with $10 million or more in annual sales. Includes information on department managers.
Million Dollar Directory Series. Dun's Marketing Services, 3 Sylvan Way, Parsippany, N.J. 07054. Over 9,000 pages in five volumes. Includes 160,000 companies along with names and titles of principal officers.

National Directory of Nonprofit Organizations. The Taft Group, 835 Penobscot Building, Detroit, Mich. 48226. Volume I lists organizations with revenues of $100,000 or more; Volume 2 lists those with revenues between $25,000 and $99,000.

Standard & Poor's Register of Corporations, Directors, and Executives. Standard & Poor's Corporation, 25 Broadway, New York, N.Y. 10004. Three volumes of over 5,000 pages. Volume 1 lists 55,000 public and private U.S. and Canadian companies, including names of officers and directors. Volumes 2 and 3 provide biographical data on 70,000 key executives and cross-references.

Thomas' Register of American Manufacturers. Thomas Publishing Company, One Penn Plaza, New York, N.Y. 10119. Profiles 152,000 manufacturers with their major products and services. Useful for locating specific product manufacturers that are not listed in any of the preceding publications.

Interviewing

In addition to books about interviewing, I have included other references that are mentioned in the text and/or that have helpful ideas for making a positive interview impression.

Carnegie, Dale. *How To Win Friends and Influence People.* New York: Simon & Schuster, 1936.

Drake, John D. *The Effective Interviewer.* New York: AMACOM Books, 1989.

Gould, Richard. *Sacked! Why Good People Get Fired and How To Avoid It.* New York: John Wiley & Sons, 1986.

Kennedy, Jim. *Getting Behind the Résumé.* Englewood Cliffs, N.J.: Prentice Hall, 1987.

Lucht, John. *Rites of Passage at $100,000+.* New York: Viceroy Press, 1988.

Medley, H. Anthony. *Sweaty Palms: The Neglected Art of Being Interviewed.* Berkeley, Calif.: Ten Speed Press, 1984.

Molloy, John T. *New Dress for Success.* New York: Warner Books, 1988.

Yeager, Neil, and Lee Hough. *Power Interviews.* New York: John Wiley, 1990.

Index